DON'T GIVE A DAMN

Dr. Bill Chun

ISBN-10: 1466369094
ISBN-13: 978-1466369092

I dedicate this book to all the women who have shaped, influenced, and enriched my life over the years.

PREFACE

Like anyone else, I've made my share of mistakes and poor choices in life. Yet somehow I've managed to achieve a degree of success and am now at a good place personally and professionally. When I reflect on what I've done right and where I've gone wrong, something interesting occurs to me: things seem to turn out best when I just don't give a damn. Allow me to explain what I mean.

When I say I don't give a damn it should not be assumed that I am careless in what I do. In fact, I am something of a perfectionist in my work and I pride myself as being as good at what I do as anyone. What I don't do is panic or let the pressure of the job get to me. I don't know how many times I've been called into surgery when some young (or sometimes not so young) surgeon has gotten into trouble and hit the panic button. Something about the atmosphere of frantic energy seems to calm me, and more often than not I'm able to resolve the issue with a combination of skill, experience, and most importantly a steady confidence. It's almost as if panic in others puts me in the zone. When all is said and done and there is a chance to decompress it feels awfully good. I'm an effective surgeon because I don't give a damn.

Owning my own practice means that I am almost as busy a small business owner as I am a physician. Business means bills and medicine means paperwork. There are always records to update, forms to submit, and bills to pay. Frankly, there isn't enough time for it all. My solution? I don't give a damn. The first and last priority for me is the well-being of my patients. Everything else comes second. Secretaries are always clamoring for records, insurance companies are always demanding forms and codes, and utility companies are always screaming for payments. I don't give a damn. Everyone gets what they need from me in due time but I refuse to panic or allow myself to be distracted from giving my patients my full and undivided attention.

As shocking as the news might be to my mother, not everyone in the world loves me. I have found that you cannot have opinions or make choices in this life without pissing off someone somewhere sometime. I don't give a damn. I make decisions that are in my own best interest and that allow me to look after the needs of my family. Why would I give a damn about anything else? Plotting, worrying, and trying to please others dilutes a person and results in a loss of focus and resolve. When a person starts to lose himself in this way he cannot be of use to others. You have an obligation to those you love to not give a damn. The important people in your life are counting on it.

Not giving a damn doesn't mean being irresponsible or selfish to the extent of harming others. On the contrary, not giving a damn is essential to being effective at your job, at peace in your life, and useful to those who depend on you. Do what is right for you—now—and you will be more effective, balanced, and reliable for yourself, your coworkers, and your loved ones. Many people are too insecure, guilt-ridden, or overwhelmed by challenges and details to be effective. They seem to think that panic indicates commitment and worrying about what others think shows thoughtfulness. They are wrong. Try it for yourself. When faced with a difficult problem, person, or situation tell yourself you don't give a damn, and believe it. Calm down, slow down, and act rationally and efficiently without unproductive anxieties. You will be surprised at how much more effective and capable you are without all the baggage that most people carry around weighing you down.

If you really care—don't give a damn.

TABLE OF CONTENTS

INTRODUCTION

I just do not give a damn, and it has made me very happy. Like everyone else, I have always had my share of challenges and trials in life; and like most people, I used to allow these to create stress and pressure that affected me significantly. In fact, I used to worry a lot about my choices in life, regret my failures, and rage at perceived affronts. Such reactions are normal and understandable, but never seemed to do me a lot of good. So I finally just stopped giving a damn, and found that I am much better off for it. In fact, everyone and everything around me is better off for it.

Looking at it one way, you could say that I have experienced quite a lot of failure in my life. I attended the US Naval Academy, but didn't finish. I was not accepted to my first choice of medical school despite my best efforts. My first two marriages ended in divorce. I have been involved in several business ventures that went nowhere. I could get pretty down on myself if I wanted to, and there was a time when I occasionally did just that. The funny thing is though, that doing so didn't help me in any way. In fact, it always turned out to be a waste of time and energy. The only thing that has ever helped me move past my failures is striding forward toward the next challenge. Not as in some dramatic movie scene where the background music grows louder and louder as the hero charges on with grim determination, but just because there's nothing else reasonable to do. I move ahead, I try again, it's just who I am. It's who everyone is if we don't allow ourselves to get 'stuck' in pointless regret and destructive self-recriminations. If we just don't give a damn.

Easier said than done, right? I haven't always found it easy to do myself. When I was younger, my emotional responses to things were quite sharp and intense. Perhaps this is an unavoidable aspect of being young. There was a time when I thought myself clever for attempting to play off my own emotions for motivation. When I felt frustration I said, "Oh no you don't!" and used that energy to double my efforts (or so I thought). When I faced failure I embraced a feeling of, "Screw you world!" and willfully twisted myself into knots, building up what I imagined was the power I needed to overcome any obstacle. Looking back now I marvel at all the energy I wasted and wonder how many decisions I made in the heat of my own passions that I might have made better with a level head.

If this kind of self-indulgence is a tendency common to the young, then I have to thank the passage of time for helping me out. You see, I didn't have any sudden burst of inspiration, I didn't climb a mountain and come down with the answers etched in stone, and I didn't receive spontaneous enlightenment from the unusual shape of a potato or something. I simply faced failure, frustration, disappointment, and hardship over and over again through the years, as we all do if we stick around long enough. Ok maybe some very lucky few don't, but the hell with them, they don't need my advice! Over time I observed that no matter how wound up I got with the highs and the lows and the worry and internalized drama, that none of it ever seemed to affect outcomes. It's like driving in city traffic. You can stand on the gas pedal with both feet between red lights or up to that next car ahead of you then slam on the brakes over and over, pounding the steering wheel and cursing out all the other drivers around you, but eventually you will notice that you get to your destination in about the same amount of time no matter how you drive. Sooner or later a wise person will settle into a reasonable pace, listen to the radio, dictate some notes, or sip on a coffee and get where they need to be calmly and in one piece. It doesn't do you any good to drive your car off the bridge in a fit of rage or, I should add, to sit in the parking lot all day afraid to put the vehicle in drive because you've been in an accident before. Sure, there are times when it makes sense to go fast, and times when you need to take the car into the shop for safety's sake, but in general just motoring on in a reasonable fashion gets you where you need to go with the least troubles and a lot less stress. Oh, and you save money on gas too.

Through observation and the passage of time I came to realize that all my anger, doubt, regret, panic, and frustration never really got me anywhere. So I stopped giving a damn. I may have come to this conclusion as a matter of necessity, not having as much energy to squander as in my youth, or it may have been the influence of my work as a surgeon, where a cool head in the midst of crisis is essential, but in any case I didn't give a damn anymore. Turns out I shouldn't have been giving a damn all along. In the following pages, I want to explain to you just what I really mean by not giving a damn. It's a simple concept, but requires some elaboration so that my meaning of the phrase is not misconstrued. Finally, I will humbly offer some suggestions as to how you can stop giving a damn and get where you need to be.

CHAPTER 1

WHAT IT MEANS TO NOT GIVE A DAMN

It's all well and good to say you don't give a damn, but what does it really mean? This is a very important question, as the phrase can be interpreted in several ways and potentially taken quite differently than how I intend it here. What I mean by "don't give a damn" may be both simpler and more positive than it seems at first glance.

⁂

Don't live in the past

In order to explain what I mean, I'd like to start with a question: Where do you live; or better yet when? If someone is accused of "living in the past," it is generally understood to be a bad thing. Someone living in the past is considered out of touch with the times, whether through choice or some inability to face reality. Such a person may be reliving past glories—or memories modified to make minor past achievements glorious—because he or she feels inadequate to create successes equal to or greater than any previous achievements, real or imagined. It's a kind of avoidance hiding behind self-flattery. In a related process, many people come to think of things in the past, aside from tragedies and personal catastrophes, as somehow better than their present circumstances. This feeling becomes stronger as time passes. Things were simpler "back then." Choices were not so confusing, or did not carry such dire consequences, and challenges did not seem so impossibly daunting. There wasn't so much stress, exhaustion, and frustration with the details of daily life. Many people come to feel this way even when their past circumstances were in fact quite trying.

Living in the past is living in an illusion. For most of us, winning that science fair, or making that last minute buzzer-beater to win the divisional basketball title, or getting the popular girl/boy to accompany us to the big dance seemed a lot more important at the time than it really was. That is not to say that certain moments in the past may not have been significant, but in perspective they are usually not what we like to feel they were. We elevate such memories because it is an easy way to feel good about ourselves without any new exertions. You don't have to squeeze into the old basketball uniform and break a sweat to feel triumphant; you just need to linger in the memory of what once was. The inclination to do so tends to increase when, over time, we start to feel that our best days may be behind us. When you feel yourself getting out of breath from climbing a short flight of stairs that star basketball player you used to be takes on the appearance and abilities of a Greek god! When you look in the mirror and see enough "extra material" hanging off your body to make a whole other person, that twenty-something you used to be starts to look like a supermodel.

Such feelings grow stronger the more negative your image of your current self grows. It becomes a self-perpetuating cycle that enables us to give up on who we are while idolizing who we think we were.

It should be noted as well that what was so very important to your sixteen year old self is probably not, in objective analysis, as earth-shattering to your current incarnation. Maybe you can't sink that three-pointer anymore, but in your current circumstances is that a relevant skill? If you are in your 50s and can't squeeze into that pink mini skirt you wore when you were 22 maybe it's just as well since that is unlikely to be the look you are going for these days. That doesn't mean that the skills and experiences gained playing basketball were a waste of time or that you didn't look just stunning in the pink mini, it just means that you are in a different part of your life here and now. This is where you need to focus your energies and attention. If you've lost that jumper, consider all the things you do today that your younger self couldn't or wouldn't. If you've outgrown that mini, perhaps you've outgrown a lot of things, and that may be for the good. Some things are meant to be outgrown.

Even if you won a gold medal in the Olympics, were awarded the Nobel Prize, and cured Cancer ten years ago you still have to live here and now, and that is where you must focus your attention. Chances are you did not do any of those things, but the point remains. Accomplishments, large and small, are great and can be a positive source of pride, comfort, and inspiration if kept in their proper perspective. Even the most minor achievements can make fond memories, but one must never rest on one's laurels no matter how grand they may be. The greatest accomplishment of yesterday does not absolve you from making choices and living your life here, now, today.

The problem with living in the

past applies to bad memories as well. Negative memories can exert an even stronger influence on our present than positive ones. There is no one, who has seen something of life, who has not suffered failures, frustration, and loss of some kind. This is an unavoidable aspect of being alive. Bad memories can remain quite vivid because of the strong emotions that are so often associated with them. We may recall in great detail a time when we felt that we had been wronged, but forget entirely the vastly greater number of times when we were treated fairly. It may be a survival instinct to remember negative experiences so that we can avoid repeating them if possible. However, it is all too easy to allow negative experiences in the past to interfere with our ability to live in the present. There is a very good reason why we have the ability to recall information and events, and it is true that those who fail to learn the lessons of the past are doomed to repeat them, but negative memories, like positive ones, need to be managed and kept in their proper perspective.

Many negative experiences are not as bad as we recall them. Unlike with good memories, time can help to put negative events in perspective for us. This effect grows stronger as more time passes. In elementary school, being embarrassed or ostracized publically may seem like the end of the world. Any adult can (or should) be able to look back and laugh at how serious it was taken by their childhood self. In high school, failure to make the varsity swim team may be absolutely devastating, but within a few years it will (or should) seem insignificant. The thrill of first love that can seem so overwhelmingly significant to the young, may be recognized as mainly the product of hormones and infatuation to a more experienced person. Of course, some negative experiences are much more serious and lasting than this, but even they need to be kept in their appropriate place. Even if you suffered terrible tragedy in the past and bear physical and mental scars that you cannot avoid you still have to live here and now, and that is where you must focus your attention. It would be callous not to recognize that some negative experiences leave lasting impressions, but even that goes to the point. The pain and repercussions must be dealt with today, not by reliving the past over and over but by making the best choices for this day, this moment. Struggling in the past does not advance the interests of the present.

While it is true that the aggregate of our past experiences contributed to who we are today, that doesn't change the fact that the only actionable reality we have is the one before us right now. All of our experiences, good and bad, have contributed to the person we are today. It is that person we have to live with and for, not the various selves that exist in our memories of different prior stages of life. Trying to live in the past is an illusion because whether we endlessly relive past glories or wallow in past failures we are still required to live today. Looking backward only prevents us from making the best choices for ourselves right here and now.

The point is that the past is past. Fond memories can be a pleasure, and even bad ones can be instructive, but the fact is that what has gone before is gone. Time seems to reach out to us along the continuum, as anyone with a mortgage can attest, but our reality and our choices are right in front of us right now. Living in the past is a trap that prevents you from embracing the only reality you have, which is the present.

⁂

Don't live in the future

While some people try to live in the past, others are overly preoccupied with the future. Both can be ways of avoiding the present. One of the dangers of living in the future is that to a certain extent it is encouraged by society. When we say that someone is living in the past, it is almost universally understood as something negative; not so with the future. The future is what we should strive for! It is where our hopes and dreams will be fulfilled and all our problems resolved! We are told to plan for the future, save for the future, race into the future. Politicians cannot stop talking about the future when they lay out their platform of lies for us. It is another trap. Preoccupation with the future can also prevent us from living in the here and now. Referring to the future is an effective way of promising—or threatening—just about anything. It is ideally suited for this because, unlike the past, it is not restricted by the inconvenience of immutable facts. People often lie about the past, but the fact is that if we can know them, there are actual events that have taken place and cannot be altered. Not so the future. We can be reasonably certain of some things, like the cycle of life and death, universal laws of physics, and predictable patterns of cause and effect. However, every so often something happens to shake even these bedrock assumptions about reality. An unsinkable ship sinks, an earthquake of a magnitude never seen before strikes, or some clever scientist discovers some small detail that throws into doubt long-held "beliefs" about the universe. It would be irrational to wake up in a panic every morning over the prospect of the Sun exploding that day. We can be reasonably certain that won't happen for a good long while. But even events and conditions about the future that we are quite sure about retain an element of the unknown. This is so because our predictions and assumptions are so often overturned, and for the simple reason that the future has not—by definition—happened yet. Uncertainty is the perfect breeding ground for illusion, manipulation, and deception.

Anyone can tell you what they intend to do in the future, and it is here that deception finds opportunity. This is a specialty of politicians. When someone promises to do this or that in the future you have the option of believing them or not. Skilled liars and manipulators can use the inherent uncertainty about the future to lead others to believe they will do things they have no intention of doing or that they know they will not be able to do. Taking it a step further, they can convince people that certain circumstances will exist in the future when they cannot reasonably make any such assurances. Sometimes those deceiving others are able to deceive themselves as well and actually believe their own assurances. Orienting yourself according to what others have convinced you they will do in the future exposes you to the risk of a great deal of wasted time and missed opportunity. Living in a future that may not come to pass prevents you from living fully in the present.

Perhaps the greatest danger in living in the future involves creating illusions of and for yourself. We all have expectations for ourselves, and we usually have hopes and plans for the future. This can be an important part of living in the present, but if managed incorrectly it can become a source of distraction, disappointment, and self-defeat. The fact that the future has not yet come to pass imbues the concept with a strong sense of potential. This potential naturally tends to impart the feeling that anything can happen in the future. To a certain extent that is correct, but only within reasonable limitations. The future is not yet written, but the chances of me becoming an Olympic diver in the next ten years are vanishingly slim. That's an extreme example of course, but the point remains. It is too easy to become attached to unrealistic or fantastic notions about what one may do or become in the future.

The potential that the future holds is not limitless in terms of practical reality. Imagination, and sometimes a desperate need to escape from who and what we really are can lead to unrealistic hopes that merely dissipate our energy instead of focusing it on the here and now. If I start running on a regular basis for health, recreation, and weight management, that is a good thing for me in the here and now. If I entertain thoughts of running in the Boston Marathon in a year or two, that can be a fun motivation for me to train and gain the aforementioned benefits of running. Lots of people run the Boston Marathon. Maybe I'll be that guy they always show on the evening news crossing the finish line by the Public Library at 8 or 9 at night. Who cares, if I have fun and get something good out of it? But if I convince myself that not only am I going to start running, not only am I going to run the Boston, but I am—at 50—going to win the race, then I am fooling myself and dispersing my energy in an unproductive way. The future is yet unwritten, but let's face it, that isn't going to happen. In fact, if I were really serious and began to train the way world-class marathon runners do, I would soon become discouraged and probably give up the whole enterprise, thereby missing out on the realistic benefits of running here and now. This would be an example of living in the future in such a manner that living for the present is undermined.

The future holds so much potential and so many opportunities that it can be difficult to focus on what is practical and realistic. This is why we must live in the present. If you want to change your career path, or start one, at any time of your life, that can be a very positive thing. However, if you simply become excited about some novel idea that does not build on your skills and experience and is not at all realistic, then you may fall into a trap that leads you from one unreasonable goal to another without the likelihood of success. This determination can be a tricky one to make, as many successful people had to try and fail over and over before finding their mark. It's a fine line between having the determination to try, try again, and simply wasting time tilting at windmills. The answer lies in the here and now. If what you are attempting makes use of the skills and experience of the person you are today, then it's worth as many tries as it takes. But if it requires unreasonable expectations of the person you are today, then it is probably a fool's errand. When you add hope, ambition, ego, and sometimes desperation into the mix, assessing the future from the standpoint of today can be difficult, but it is important enough to get it right. Getting it wrong not only invites disappointment and wastes time and energy, but leaves you vulnerable to con men and other manipulators.

Caution against living in the future should not be taken to mean a disregard for setting goals and planning ahead. Setting goals does not mean living in the future. In fact, it can be one of the most effective ways of ensuring that you live in the present. Setting realistic goals should involve doing what is best for you today in the understanding that it will lead to a certain outcome. However, the focus must be on the "today" part, not on the future outcome. This is important. If you have weight loss goals—reasonable ones determined through consultation with your physician—that involve your exercising a certain amount of time each week or limiting your caloric intake each day, you should do that exercise and limit those calories not on behalf of the outcome you are hoping for but because it is the right thing for you to do for yourself today. If you take care of today, those goals and more will come. This is managing the future without becoming trapped in it. If your ultimate goal is to lose 40 pounds and you weigh yourself every day with that 40 pounds hanging over your head you will likely become discouraged and give up at some point. If you focus on the half a pound you lost today and accept that as the victory it is, your long-term goal will get here by and by.

The same notion applies to any goal or planning. If you are interested in acquiring new or expanded skills in order to advance or change your career, you need to focus on what you can learn today and how that benefits you in the here and now. Of course the goal is still there, but if you sit with your elbow propped up on a text book dreaming of that future job you will get nowhere. Put your nose in that book and learn all you can right now because it will make you more informed and valuable in the marketplace today. When you go to sleep at night you should not be dreaming of that long or even short-term goal, you should ask yourself what you did today to make yourself better today. If you are unsatisfied with that answer then get up and get back to it because those other goals will never materialize otherwise. Make the future, like the past, now. And don't give a damn about your ally instead of your enemy by keeping the focus squarely on the here and anything else.

Live in the present

Some people find the present intimidating. When you truly live in the present there is no place to hide. You can't pretend to be what you once were (or thought you were), and you can't wander off into unrealistic fantasies about what you imagine you could be. You have to deal with yourself, your life, and your responsibilities right here, right now. So much of the stress, worry, and trouble that we make for ourselves stems from a failure to simply embrace the present. For all the negative consequences that doing so brings, it is amazing how eager many people are to avoid the present. It's like a child who thinks that if he closes his eyes the world, rather than just his ability to see it, will go away along with whatever it is he would like to avoid. Sadly, for many people this same exercise involves escaping into drugs and alcohol, which of course only compounds whatever problems one would like to hide from anyway. For too many Americans, food functions just like a drug in this way. The answer lies, of course, in not avoiding the present.

Worry is not a part of living in the moment. Worry involves undue concern over things which cannot be controlled. It is a form of living in the future, and a waste of energy. If things can be controlled then action, not worry, is the appropriate response. If they cannot be controlled then there is no point in wasting energy on them. We should focus instead on making the best choices for ourselves in this moment. Regret is similar to worry. It is a form of living in the past and also involves wasting energy on things that cannot be changed. Both worry and regret are common means of avoiding the present. Many people believe that these are feelings that descend upon them from the outside, but the fact is that they are generated and sustained from within. This means that we can make better decisions than to allow the past and the future to dissipate our energy; we can choose to not give a damn and just live in the here and now. You've made mistakes in the past? Who hasn't? Once you have restored what was broken, and mended fences as much as reasonably possible, it is time to leave that mistake behind and focus on what is in front of you. If others choose to harbor grudges or permanently define you by some past mistake that is their problem. Your business is with the present. A plane flying to Chicago could possibly crash. Does that mean you don't take that trip you've been planning? If the trip was the right decision for you to make in the first place, you go and don't give a damn about things you cannot control. If you go outside, you could get hit by a bus or contract an illness and die. Should you therefore hide inside and never breathe fresh air, get dirty, and embrace life? Nonsense. If there is something outside worth doing you do it. If it's the best choice for you right now, apply for that job, take a chance on that new romance, or make that investment without being a prisoner of worry.

Living in the present makes some people nervous because they have been conditioned to pay undue concern to the past and the future. One may feel untethered by leaving the past where it belongs. Another may feel somehow "irresponsible" if not constantly fretting over the future. Changing one's attitude or orientation can be unsettling, but the end result is actually very liberating. Living every day for that day, with a clear mind and a sharp focus made possible by eliminating illusions, distractions, and pointless worries or regrets is empowering and can instill a new confidence in all you do. One of the first things you will notice when you stop giving a damn is how mired those around you are in the unnecessary things you have just freed yourself from. With a bright eye and a light mind you may say to yourself, "I used to be like that." You don't have to be like that. No one does.

CHAPTER 2

YOU ARE ALIVE AND YOU ARE GOING TO DIE

An important part of not giving a damn involves truly embracing something that should be obvious: as human beings, each of us is alive now and each of us will die one day. Fully accepting this is not as easy as it may seem. Think about it, how often do you stop to really consider the fact that you are a living organism and what that means? And not just any old organism, but a human being capable of thought, emotion, and creativity of a kind seen nowhere else in nature. You may or may not be a religious person, but if the word "miracle" means anything, then you are surely one. When was the last time you allowed yourself to be aware of your own breathing, thinking, and feeling at a given moment? Most of us rush through each day too busy, tired, or frustrated for such considerations. Part of living for the present is being aware of who and what we are; right here and right now. It is not a waste of time to reflect upon yourself, if only for a short time, and there is nothing wrong with allowing yourself to feel joy at just being alive.

Of course the other side of realizing that you are truly alive is recognizing that you are going to die one day. An inescapable part of the deal when you are born is that you will one day expire. People of various faiths believe in an afterlife of some kind, and if that brings them comfort then that is all well and good, but I am referring here to physical death. The human body has a limited lifespan. Throughout history people have tended to really struggle with this one. Death is feared, ignored, avoided, or denied through a variety of concepts. In order to truly not give a damn you have to recognize your mortality and accept it. To put it bluntly, we could, any of us, drop dead at any given moment. Stroke, heart attack, lightning strike, city bus, or any of a number of events could call the game short at any time. Longer, even less pleasant processes such as terminal illness can also begin at any time. As I've said, many people rely on religious belief systems to help them cope with this reality, but even in the absence of such faith the inevitability and random potential of death should not instill fear. Accepting this reality is essential to not giving a damn.

⁂

Make this moment fit to be your last

You cannot truly live in the moment unless you are prepared to have that moment be your last. For many people, the initial reaction to such a notion is emotional and extreme. They talk of performing any of a number of rash, dangerous, or irrational acts on their last day or in their last moment. Upon more thoughtful reflection, however, most people settle down and start to think about what is most important to them. At this point responses turn to being with loved ones and reflecting on what is most important in their lives. Here we start to see the point of living in the moment.

If you were going to die in an hour you would try to spend that time with the ones you love, so try in your everyday life to spend as much time as possible with the ones you love. The ones you love are not a video game, the internet, your cell phone, or a bar. If the task you are doing at work were to be the last piece of work you would be remembered by you would try to make it your best. If the last thing you could do to your body were something to honor it, or to pollute it, which would you choose? If your last thoughts could be clear and peaceful, or clouded and impaired, which would you want to be the last that send you to eternity? You can do something this day and this moment to make your mind clear and peaceful. Would you rather wallow in doubt, fear, and regret? Would you rather dull your senses to the point that you cannot fully experience your last moment? You can do something this day and this moment to make your body healthier and stronger. Would you rather spend your last moments lamenting over the body you used to have and feeling regret at how your body will be viewed in posterity? You can do something this day and this moment to let those you love know how you really feel. Would you rather have grudges, unresolved issues, and missed opportunities be your final connection? You can do something this day and this moment to honor who you are and what you do. Would you rather be remembered for your own sake as one who left things unfinished or didn't do your very best all the time? The finite quality of our lives can be a very positive motivator if we learn how to let it be instead of fearing and hiding from our mortality.

✖ ✖ ✖

Accept both life and death

Embracing life and death is essential for being able to live in the present and not give a damn. When you focus on the special value of being alive and embrace the inevitability and unpredictability of death, can you really be bothered to give a damn what those who are not your loved ones think about you? Can the little annoyances and frustrations of everyday life mean anything in comparison? Do you have the time for worry or regret? Is there any reason to make any decision but the one that is best for you right here and right now? Why give a damn?

CHAPTER 3

PRIORITIES

Now that we've established that not giving a damn involves making the best decisions for you in the here and now, the question must be asked, "What are the best decisions?" Such a general question is difficult to answer with specificity, but we can recognize some useful guidelines that can be applied to a variety of situations.

⁂

Is a decision grounded in the present?

The best decisions are the ones made in and for the here and now. An awareness of the present, and an understanding of the traps of both past and future, is necessary to make such decisions. Of course it is reasonable to take into account prior experiences when making decisions in the present. No need to put your hand on a hot stove four or five times before deciding that is an unproductive course of action. But when you think about it, you never really needed to burn your hand in the first place, did you? A reasonable decision in the present would take into account an understanding that the stove is hot and can burn things like a hand. This decision takes into account knowledge about stoves and hands such that the proper choices can be made without suffering burns. Maybe somewhere along the line somebody had to burn his hand, but we can benefit from his experience without reliving it or ignoring it.

If a decision is based on a fear from the past, it is not of the here and now. Perhaps you tried to accomplish something in the past and failed. If the original attempt was based on a reasonable assessment of viability, then that failure need not be taken as an indication that the attempt was impossible or improbable. It would then follow that it is not unrealistic to attempt something similar again if present conditions suggest a reasonable likelihood of success. To avoid making a reasonable decision or taking a calculated risk based on the fear of a previous failure is to allow yourself to be trapped in the past. This is most certainly not living in the here and now.

If you applied for a certain job for which you felt you had the requisite skills and experience but failed to get the position, it does not hold that you should not apply for a similar job again if the opportunity presents itself. If you tried to lose weight in the past and failed, it does not mean you shouldn't make healthy choices for yourself today. If you have loved and lost you must not hide from love the next time it knocks on your door. Of course, if some past failure was the result of wild speculation or exaggerated enthusiasm, then it is wise to remember and learn from that mistake. Living in the here and now does not mean repeating mistakes of the past endlessly. If you for some reason applied for a job for which you had no applicable skills, training, or experience and were rejected, it would be a waste of time to apply again. If your affections for a person were unambiguously spurned, it would be best to move on rather than trying to 'win' their love. However, avoiding the best decision for you today because of a painful experience in the past means allowing yourself to be shackled by the past rather than informed by it.

Basing present decisions on past successes can also lead you astray. The fact that you have managed to do something in the past does not necessarily indicate that you can or should do the same thing again. Circumstances may have changed such that what was accomplished in the past is not likely or advisable in the present. What was a successful choice at one time may be the very worst decision now. Making the decision to do something now just because you were successful at it sometime before can lead to grievous error. Successful strategies employed by a leader in a time of war may be the worst approach for that same leader in a time of peace or even in a different war that presents different circumstances. A business approach that reaped great rewards once might only invite ruin if attempted under market conditions that have changed in the interim. Repeating the same action for no other reason than that it was once successful is a sure way of proving that it will not always be so.

The key is to make the right decision for today, not for yesterday. There should be no shame involved in admitting that there are some things you could accomplish once that you cannot accomplish now, just as there are things you can do now that you could not do before. My 50 year-old self cannot play soccer the way my 16 year-old self could, and it would be a comical mistake to try, but it would have been a much worse disaster if my 16 year-old self had attempted to perform surgery the way that I can today. I would not trade that past success for the present one, and it turns out I have no choice in the matter anyway. Good decisions are not based on what I could once do, but on what I can and should do right here, right now. There is nothing wrong with building on past successes and accumulating skills and experience, but your choices must be for and of today, not yesterday. An experienced boxer cannot fight the way he did when he was starting out and would be a fool to try, even if he enjoyed great success then. A smart fighter makes use of his ring experience instead of trying to be a kid forever. Reality will have it no other way. The right choices for who and what you are today should not be hindered by who and what you once were, even if past experience was quite positive. Turning success in the past into a failure of the present would be unfortunate and unnecessary.

If a decision is based on regret about the past, it is not of the here and now. We have established that regret is largely a waste of time. It stands to reason that decisions made under the influence of such a distraction are unlikely to be good ones. Feelings of regret can lead to decisions that are attempts to make up for something that has come before. This will not only fail to have the intended effect, but will almost certainly create further problems. Regret is a waste of time primarily because it involves focusing undue attention on events or decisions that are unalterably complete in the past. Making decisions due to or based on regret can lead all too easily to becoming trapped in the past.

If a decision is based on fear of the future, it is not of the here and now. The uncertainty inherent in considerations of the future is also the source of its limitless potential. This potential can, and does, manifest in both positive and negative ways. While many people are lured by dreams of the future, others are frightened into inactivity by what might be. Falling into the trap of fearing the future results in an unproductive aversion to risk and an exaggerated fear of failure or catastrophe. Making the right decision for you right now involves accepting a degree of uncertainty and understanding that there will always be factors and events outside of our control. Without accepting a degree of risk in life we could never get out of bed or put one foot in front of the other. How much and what type of risk is acceptable will differ for each individual and circumstance, that's why you can't give damn what anyone else thinks you should do. You may consider wise and well intentioned counsel, but at the end of the day you are the one making the choices and you are the one living with the consequences. A clear and honest assessment of the choices available to you right now cannot take place if you are trapped in a fear of the future.

If a decision is based on ungrounded fantasy about the future, it is not of the here and now. As unproductive as an undue fear of the future are unrealistic expectations. One of the traditional strengths of America as a nation and a people has been a powerful "can do" spirit. A certain degree of fearless optimism was necessary to settle the West, send a man to the Moon, and risk everything in the Cold War. However, at the same time we slaughtered Native Americans, invented the atomic bomb, and have made more than a few bad gambles in international affairs. The point is that the line between great accomplishments and great disasters is a fine one. Just as nothing can be accomplished if we are frozen by a fear of the future, we can make a real mess of things if we are unrealistic about what we can and should do. Just where this line falls will differ for each individual and circumstance, that's why you can't give a damn what anyone else thinks. What seems a great opportunity in business, love, or personal well-being to one person may appear to be sheer folly to another and they may both be correct. Each individual's abilities, goals, and circumstances will inform their own decision about what is right for them here and now.

⌘⌘⌘

Is a decision the best one for you?

Most people have had friends, teachers, and mentors who have helped to shape and inform their knowledge and outlook on the world and who have therefore made a significant impression on them. Good advice from trusted, well-meaning, and qualified sources can be a great help in determining the best decision for any given moment. However, the focus of the decision-making process must be the self. Sometimes it may seem easier to surrender responsibility for making decisions and just do whatever you are told, but you cannot surrender responsibility for the consequences of those choices (provided you are an adult in full command of your faculties). The best choice for you right now can only come from you, and ownership of poor choices can only rest with you. You may be thinking at this point that there are others in your life who share in the consequences of your decisions and whose interests and point of view must also be taken into account. We will expand on the concept of "you" in a later section.

⁂

Is it a decision you could accept as your last?

Ultimately, we live in this moment because as far as we know any moment could be our last. Every decision should be made with this in mind. Would you want the very last decision you ever make to be one that is reckless or irresponsible? That befouls or dishonors your body? A decision based on fear or spite or anger? Or would you want that final decision to be one that reflects all the best of who you were for yourself and your loved ones? When every decision is approached this way, a very positive life emerges.

CHAPTER 4

DON'T GIVE A DAMN ABOUT MONEY

Money. They say it is the root of all evil, but then they also say it makes the world go 'round. I say don't give a damn about it.

In trying economic times, it can be a real challenge to meet all of one's obligations and manage to live in relative comfort. In fact, sometimes it's downright impossible. Bills come in and prices go up regardless of a given individual's financial situation. The loss of a job, a sudden illness or accident, or the unexpected departure of a wage earner from the household can easily throw a precarious budget into utter turmoil. Such a situation can have a strongly negative effect on many areas of life if allowed to do so. Money is one of the chief causes of stress and related ills in many people's lives. Or so many people think. They are mistaken.

Stress does not come from without, but from within, and that is where it needs to be addressed. Whether the cause is money, love, or the challenges involved in getting older, stress is something created, nurtured, and all too often grown to dangerous dimensions from the inside out. It is common to think of stress as an unavoidable reaction to forces from the outside coming in, but that is not accurate. Our reactions to external events are our choice; we just have to make the right one for any given moment. That's why we should not give a damn about money.

⁂

How to not give a damn about money

Now, it's all well and good to say, "I don't give a damn about money," but when the bills are piling up and the wolf is at the door it can be easier said than done. Start by putting it all in perspective. Those bills really are just pieces of paper. They are not going to bite you if you open them, and the information on them is not going to go away if you hide from them and don't open your mail for weeks at a time. Face them, organize them, prioritize them, but don't fear them. Rest assured, if you can't pay one of them on time, they will send out another.

I would never recommend not paying your bills on time, because that can be even more costly in the long run. However, if the decision facing you right now is one of feeding your family tonight or avoiding that dreaded third late notice, it should be a very simple one.

Making the right decision for you right now is the key to dealing with financial matters just as it is to dealing with the entire range of issues that affect our lives. Without becoming trapped by regrets about the past or anxiety over the future, each of us should base our actions on a clear and reasonable evaluation of what is the best choice among those facing us right now.

⁂

Realize what is and is not the right choice

A useful first step involves realizing just what is and is not part of making the right choice. Consider the choice of what you will eat for lunch. Do you decide what to have based on what you think you "must" eat to impress your neighbors? Of course not. Would you eat something you know will kill you just because you are told that everyone else is eating it and you don't want to be left behind? Ridiculous. Sure, many of us occasionally eat unhealthy food that we probably shouldn't, but that is in spite of what we know to be the best decision. If we think about what is best for our body we will not eat so much that we can't possibly digest all that we have consumed.

Financial matters are similar. When you are in the moment of making a decision about whether or not to purchase something, if impressing others is a controlling factor then it is probably not the best decision you could make. These "others" will not be making use of the item, you will. They will not bear the financial responsibility for the decision, you will. Unless you are in a position where impressing others stands to directly benefit you financially, the best decision is usually the most practical one. Paying to impress people who for the most part (let's be honest) couldn't care less about your "image" is a poor allocation of resources. Likewise, making a non-essential purchase that you know you cannot afford is unlikely to be the best decision you could make. There are many forces at work in society today that encourage consumption for its own sake. It would seem obvious that such behavior is ill-considered, but those forces come into play most strongly at the very moment of purchase, preying upon impulses to encourage a given action rather than careful thinking. This is the moment when you need to exercise control over your emotions and focus on the most rational decision for you right now.

⁂

Make the right decision for right now

Of course if you really don't give a damn that moment is every moment, because the only moment you need to act upon is the one you are in. In fact, the only moment in your life that you can control directly is this one. Make the right decision for this moment and you will start stringing together many right decisions very soon. In this way, positive trends begin to emerge. The person who can stay the course and keep making the best decisions for right now will enjoy the most positive consequences of those decisions over the long term.

When people find themselves, for whatever reason, in precarious financial straits, it can seem as if there are no good decisions. The walls start closing in and there are hands grabbing from every direction making - on insufficient resources. Financial calamity, loss of reputation, and even the threat of legal action loom ominously overhead. It is understandable that so many people surrender to panic, despair, or even depression in the face of such a formidable array of negative forces. It is understandable, but unnecessary.

Panic, despair, and depression are very unlikely to ever resolve an economic (or any other) problem. In fact, giving in to these self-generated opponents is very likely to make problems much worse. When we allow our emotions to control us rather than vice versa, we become less likely to make clear, rational decisions for and in the here and now. Powerful, uncontrolled emotions lead us into traps. We may become wrapped up in feelings of regret or guilt over what has come before, or we may become trapped in fear and anticipation over what we think lies ahead. As we have discussed previously, traps of the past or the future can prevent us from making the best choices right now. Even when people manage to ground themselves in the present, panic or hopelessness (remnants of the aforementioned traps) can encourage poor decision making. Unfortunately, economic difficulties tend to inspire such unproductive reactions in many people. Perhaps this is because money issues seem like something so crucial to our lives but so much outside of our control.

Financial matters are not, of course, outside of our control. Like anything else in our lives, they are subject to our own decision-making. We need to approach them by keeping a clear mind, controlling our emotions, and making the best decision right now. Make no mistake, when it comes to money the best choice is not always the easiest one and the distinction between what we want and what we need can become all too easily blurred. However, if we really don't give a damn what anyone else thinks and are able to avoid the traps along the way, we can always make the right choice right now.

Depending on one's individual situation, the right choice may or may not include the following suggestions.

⁂

Destroy the credit card

While credit cards can useful and convenient financial tools when used the right way and very carefully managed, they are also very dangerous. It's like carrying a hand grenade in your pocket with the pin pulled out. If you walk a certain way so as to keep the striker lever tight you'll be ok and if for some reason you ever need a grenade there's nothing better, but make one mistake and...you get the idea. And really, how often are you going to need a hand grenade that it could possibly justify the risk? Interest rates and penalty triggers on credit cards are as destructive and unforgiving as a bomb. Get your scissors and destroy that explosive financial device. For all but the largest purchases, you will likely find that you can do without the card. Only spending what you can actually afford right now is almost always a good decision. Purchases which for most of us are almost always based on credit to some degree, like homes and automobiles, are rarely credit card transactions. The risk to reward ratio (when reward is understood as a "need" rather than a "want") weighs strongly against credit cards. Like a reformed smoker, after a few months you will be amazed at how good you feel and how much money you've saved by removing this carcinogen from your life.

Stop eating out

We have to eat, but we don't have to eat out. Eating out can be fun, convenient, and even cheap, but it's bad for you in many ways. Eating out at a "sit down" restaurant can be a refreshing, rewarding break from the norm—when it makes sense to do so. Considering the time and expense involved, it rarely makes sense to do so. Think about how many costs are associated with such an activity. Compare the time that must be allocated to eating out compared with that of eating at home. There is the time spent preparing to go out, the time spent traveling to the destination, the meal itself (waiting for a table, waiting on wait staff, etc.), returning home, and decompressing from the experience. Think about how much time eating out consumes as compared to dinner at home. If time is money, that's a pretty big bill.

Eating out is less healthy than eating at home. Even when eating out "healthy" (non-fast food), you are likely to consume more salt, fat, and calories than what you would have prepared for yourself at home. Even when it becomes a fairly regular occurrence, eating out is considered by many as something "special" and therefore our normal concern for what and how much we eat is set aside. The consequences to this kind of eating can add up quickly. Although the phrase "eating out" conjures up images of candle-lit dinners attended to by fawning wait- staff, the fact is that for most of us most of the time it means grabbing quickly prepared, ready-made food. You don't need me to tell you that fast food is some of the most harmful stuff you can put into your body. You also don't need me to tell you that it's cheap, convenient, and often pretty tasty. There's a reason why fast food places are so successful; these businesses are good at what they do. Unfortunately, what fast food does is poison people. There are mountains of scientific evidence as to the harmful effects of such food. This evidence is largely unnecessary however, as anyone who has consumed fast food will be familiar with the sick, bloated feeling that follows. The fact that a lot of this kind of food is very cheap can be a lure when money is tight, but in the long run it can be quite costly to your health.

Eating out is an unnecessary expense. As much as it is a waste of time, it is equally a waste of money. Eating out involves transportation costs, even if it is a minor detour on the way home from work. If food is delivered the lack of transportation cost is offset by tips and delivery fees. Going out to a "sit down" restaurant obviously involves traveling to and from the location, often paying for parking, overpriced food, tips, and perhaps drinks. It all adds up to a great deal more than preparing a simple, healthy meal at home. If you are in a position where you can afford all of these costs and you determine that right now that money is not better spent on or saved for something else, once in a while it can't hurt to treat yourself and your family. However, it can be all too easy to fall into a habit of eating out, be it at a restaurant, having a pizza delivered, or fast food. Before you know it, the expense starts to take its toll. Fast food would seem to contradict this advice since it is often so cheap. Note that I said "cheap" not "inexpensive." By ordering off the "value menu" at one of many fast food chains, it is possible to fill bellies with remarkably little money. However, this is not without additional cost. Making the best decision for you in the here and now will very rarely involve actively harming yourself. Deciding to put something into your body that you know for certain is bad for you cannot be the best possible choice. You don't need to worry about being overweight ten years from now if you decide to put something healthy in your body right now instead of gorging on fat and carcinogens. That value menu is not such a value when you consider the cost of being unhealthy. Buying ever-larger clothes, prescription medications, and potential hospitalizations are not inexpensive and are a very real consequence of making the wrong choice right now.

⋆⋆⋆

Simplify your life

All of the "conveniences" and "advances" of the modern world tend to clutter our minds, our spirits, and our lives in general. Look around your home and ask yourself how much of all that you possess you truly could not live without. Sit down and make a list. If you are honest with yourself you will end up with a very short list. Everything not on your list is costing you in one way or another. If you start the process of eliminating everything from your life that is not on your list you may be surprised at the effect it has on you. Physically removing things from your life that you do not need (recycle, donate, or gift) lightens the heart and clears the mind. The feeling of becoming "cleaner" with every unnecessary item discarded can become addictive. We are so frantically overloaded with information, electronics, entertainment, and superfluous material goods that shedding them is startlingly refreshing. You don't need to know everything at every moment, you don't need to have every "new" device (which will be obsolete in a few months) and you don't need to have the latest fashion in order to keep covered up. All these things are a drain on your consciousness as surely as they are on your wallet.

⁂

Downsize as circumstances dictate

Not only is it a good idea to simplify your life, sometimes it is an absolute must. Rather than sinking into even more unsustainable debt, it is sometimes necessary to take a few steps back down the economic ladder. Not giving a damn means making the best choice among those available to you without concern for the opinions of others and without becoming trapped by your own emotions. When economic times are really tough you might have to do without the "extras" for a while. This could mean not buying any new clothes for some time, or doing without a TV. It is possible to do and the world doesn't come to an end just because there isn't constant background noise from the television 24 hours a day. If push comes to shove you may have to sell the car and start taking the bus. Such a decision shouldn't be perceived as shocking or extreme. If you sit down and consider your situation carefully and clearly and conclude that selling your car is the best decision for right now then that is what you should do. There need not be any undue emotion involved. If you have to sell your house and move into an apartment, or move from your current apartment into a smaller one then that is what you do. The best choice for your current economic circumstances should be the only concern. If things get so difficult that you have to visit the local food pantry and/or apply for food stamps then that is what you should do if it is the best, or only, choice for you for right now. Financial problems don't go away, but they can be managed if you don't give a damn.

⁂

Set pride aside

For many of us, the thought of selling the house and moving into a small apartment or seeking food assistance seems extreme and even shameful, but it isn't if you don't give a damn. Needless to say, one would only make such decisions if it were truly necessary. However, some decisions that are clearly necessary are avoided out of stubborn pride. Many people would rather slide further and further into crushing debt rather than look clear-ly at the best options in front of them. Pride is an emotion that is too often influenced by giving a damn. If what you consider pride is really an undue concern about what others might think about the choices you have to make for yourself (and your extended "self"), you have fallen into a trap. No one has to live with the consequences of your choices the way you do. The benefit of not giving a damn is that it allows you to think clearly and to maintain control over your emotions. Pride is what you should feel when you know you have made the right decisions to allow you to care for yourself and your family the best way possible. By making a series of right decisions right now you will set positive trends in motion and can expect your situation to improve, bit by bit and step by step. That is something to be proud of.

It's easy to offer such advice, but what we tend to think of as pride can be difficult to overcome. This tends to land people in trouble time and time again. Like any other emotion pride by itself is not an inherently negative thing, but like any other emotion it is only useful when you control it rather than being controlled by it. If you don't like taking the bus you shouldn't go out and by a car you can't afford. You should focus on working hard and being frugal until you can afford one realistically. That is something to be proud of. Clearing the clutter from your life and your mind can help make these decisions easier. It takes stamina, honesty, and control to not give a damn, but more often than not, things will pick up if you stay the course (the right one for you).

So open those bills, organize them, prioritize them, and consider your situation clearly. Then make the best decisions for right now and don't give a damn about anything else.

CHAPTER 5

DON'T GIVE A DAMN ABOUT WEIGHT LOSS

Many people want to lose weight, but many more only *say* they do. Perhaps it would be more accurate to say that they want to want to lose weight. There would be a lot less frustration over it if they just stopped giving a damn.

For most people, barring certain ailments or conditions, losing weight is not terribly complicated. If you burn more calories than you take in, you will lose weight. If you take in more calories than you burn, you will gain weight. Ok, the details are bit more complicated than that, but you get the idea. Exercising more plus eating less generally equals losing weight for most people. The hard part comes in actually putting this simple equation into action. Of course it's not really "hard" if you don't give a damn. Few things are.

⁂

Make a real decision

One of the biggest reasons why so many people fail in their attempts at losing weight is that they never really decide to. This is because so many people misunderstand what it means to make a decision. Many of us confuse wanting something with deciding to do something. It's all too easy a mistake to make and it usually results in frustration and disappointment, two emotions that run contrary to not giving a damn.

We want to be thinner, we want to save money, we want to have better relations with our loved ones, etc. Of course we want these things; they are positive and valuable things to achieve. However, merely wanting something produces no effect towards achieving it. I may wake up one day and want to go to the Moon. It requires almost nothing of me to want to go there, but actually getting there is another story.

✠✠✠

Real decisions require action

Deciding to do something—really deciding—involves action. This is where things get a bit trickier. A decision that is not coupled with action is just desire, fantasy, or self-deception. All decisions, as we know, are made of, for, and in the here and now. The thing about living in and for the moment is that there is always another moment coming up. This is obvious but important. Decisions must involve action and that action must be sustained long enough for something to actually happen. Think about how easy it is to start a project but never finish it. How many great ideas have died only half-realized throughout history? How many world-altering endeavors have been left undone? Humanity's ability to squander oppotunity is truly unique. If something really is the right decision for right now it must be the right decision for many right nows. If it's not the right decision for long enough to accomplish it, then it wasn't really the right decision at all. This is why a clear mind and careful, honest consideration are essential to the decision making process.

⁂

Real decisions require commitment

Deciding to do something involves commitment. It's easy to like the idea of doing something, but more difficult to accept the obligation of commitment. This obligation is to oneself. People often honestly feel bad when they let down someone else by failing to meet their obligation, but the truth is we get over that sort of thing pretty quickly. There is nothing more existentially eroding than failing an obligation to yourself. This is why so many of us avoid making such obligations. It's too much pressure. We don't want to fail ourselves, so it's much easier not to try; to hold ourselves to low expectations. The problem is that nothing much of any significance is accomplished that way. It's good not to give a damn what other people think, but it's hard not to give a damn what you think. Some of the world's greatest athletes perform out of a fear of losing. They know that they are capable of performing at an extraordinary level, and if they don't push themselves as hard as they ever have they will know that they have failed themselves. Many people fail to realize their full potential for just this reason. If they push themselves as fully and honestly as they can—at anything—they will be required to do so again and again because inside they will know what to measure future efforts against.

All this sure sounds like giving a damn, but it needn't. When you can commit yourself to something fully, and truly accept that there is no going back, you can relax and focus on making the right actions based on the right decisions in light of that commitment in every given moment. Accepting and internalizing this commitment honestly is the key. Although when all is said and done we really can't, we try awfully hard to fool ourselves sometimes. Many an internal pep talk merely masks the fact that a full commitment has not been made. We want to believe we have made a commitment to ourselves when we know, somewhere deep inside, that we really have not. There is a danger involved in this, because when we fail to truly decide often enough we start to lose faith in ourselves. Our expectations for ourselves start to fall, and soon we don't have a whole lot of respect for ourselves. Hard to get anything done that way. The good news is that as hard as bad habits are to break, so are good ones. The more often you keep your word to yourself the more you trust and respect yourself. Even if you have failed yourself over and over again in the past you will find that you are remarkably forgiving to the person closest to you. Positivity breeds positivity. Over time, it becomes easier to make clear decisions and see them through. Once you've mastered the decision making process the rest is just a matter of completing the steps.

⁂

Make realistic decisions

In order to reach this level of comfortable commitment within yourself you need to be realistic about what you decide to do. If you truly decide to leap over a bus you are going to fail no matter how sincere you are. Repeated failure due to unrealistic goals can set the whole negative set of conditions in motion as referenced above. It is therefore important to choose carefully and realistically what you decide to do. This means, of course, that every such choice will be different for every individual. Many people make the mistake of trying to adopt the choices that are right for others instead of evaluating clearly and honestly what is the best choice for themselves. The right decision cannot be made based on the best choice for some-one else. Consider what is best for you and don't give a damn about anyone else.

Here the notion of "anyone else" needs some clarification. We have repeated quite often by now that the right decision for right now needs to be made by you and for you. In the following section we will elabo-rate on the notion of "you" and how it fits into our decision making proc-ess. Suffice to say that "you" very often involves more than one per-son. "Anyone else" falls outside an expanded notion of "you."

⁂

Losing weight

You may have noticed that we have not talked a lot about actually losing weight so far. That's because dropping the pounds is the easy part. It doesn't always feel easy, but compared to fully accepting and internalizing the decision to lose weight, it's a snap. There are a seemingly endless number of diet programs out there and here's the thing: almost all of them work. If you stick to any program that restricts your caloric intake, you are likely to lose weight. The key doesn't lie in the particulars of the program but in the ability of the individual to stay the course. This is why it all comes down to really deciding to lose the weight. The rest are really just details. Some diets are of questionable nutritional value, and others involve a good deal of superfluous 'ideology,' but as long as they involve controlling and restricting calories (hopefully with increased exercise as well) they will result in weight loss sooner or later. It's about the decision, not the details. People who have had success with this or that diet extol its virtues and encourage everyone they know to try it, but they are missing the point. You cannot make that all important decision for someone else and without it nothing will be effective. "It" doesn't work, you do.

This is not to say that people cannot positively influence one another when it comes to weight loss (or anything else). Losing weight or starting an exercise regimen with a partner can be encouraging, and reinforce positive steps. The key here is to find a person who has made the same decision that you have. Mutual support is most effective when both parties have the same goals and level of commitment. If one starts to waver the other can serve as a reminder of the similar decisions they have made. However, if one party at some point makes a different decision, or was never fully committed to start with, then all the encouragement in the world is unlikely to be persuasive. It is unfortunately rare to find a weight loss partner who truly shares the same attitude and commitment, that's why the bottom line remains not giving a damn about what anyone else may decide but you. If you do find an appropriate partner, the results and relationship can be very rewarding.

A weight loss mentor or guide can also be a positive influence on the process. Someone who has been through the process you are involved in often has valuable insights that you may or may not choose to accept. The key to an appropriate guide is that he or she understands the role. This role is not to force you along their way, but to help you along your way. An effective guide knows that the only right way is your way. Unfortunately, it can be difficult to find a guide who really understands this role and does not attempt to impose their own will in place of yours. This type of control is unlikely to be successful because you can't accomplish your own goals unless you don't give a damn.

Avoid the traps

As we have reiterated several times now, not giving a damn means making the right choice for you right here and now. Many people fail in their weight loss efforts because they fall into the traps of the past or future. If you have failed at attempts to lose weight in the past, you may become discouraged and feel as if your every effort is doomed to failure. This is allowing a past failure to control your present. If you never had a problem losing weight before, you may be falsely confident that doing so now will be effortless. Many people become trapped by past success this way when they fail to take into account how their bodies, habits, and circumstances have changed over time. This trap often leads to rude awakenings. As we have discussed previously, the future holds traps as well. Sometimes people are so convinced that they will fail or that after having achieved their goals they will "inevitably" rebound, that they hold themselves back and do not commit fully to the goal they say they want to pursue. Other times people will set such unrealistic goals that they all but guarantee failure and frustration. "I will lose 100 pounds in a month!" is not a goal, it is a delusion. Such delusions are often a means of avoiding the real work and commitment involved in pursuing a realistic goal.

⁂

Focus on the step right in front of you

They say that the journey of 1000 miles begins with a single step. That step should be all you are concerned with. If you try to look at the goal 1000 miles away you will stand frozen and squinting at the horizon to no avail. This step, right now is the only one you will ever need to worry about. Take that step, do it well, and you'll see that the very same challenge is still in front of you. That one step is where you need to focus your attention. Instead of obsessing over a number or living on top of the scale, focus on the choices in front of you right now. What are you going to eat, or not eat, for this meal? Are you going to drink an extra glass of water right now? Could you be exercising in some fashion at this moment? If you are clear-eyed and honest with yourself it is not difficult to see which choices will move you closer to your goal and which ones will not. Make the best choice for you right now without worrying about that destination 1000 miles away and before you know it you'll be closer than you could have imagined. It's good to have goals as long as you don't let them have you. If it seems that someone else is making faster progress, or no one notices how far you've come—just don't give a damn. You'll reach your goals your way in your time.

One major concern with any diet or weight loss program is maintaining your progress once you've made it. If you continue to focus on the best choices for you in the present the way you did to reach your goal, you can't help but maintain those gains and continue to build upon them. Focusing on what is best for you here and now is not really about losing weight, though that may be a happy consequence; it is about living directly, honestly, and positively every moment of your life. Good things cannot help but flow from that.

CHAPTER 6

DON'T GIVE A DAMN ABOUT LOVE

Ah, love; that great intangible that has inspired poetry, instigated wars, and caused all manner of noble and ridiculous behavior throughout human history. It occupies our minds and stirs our hearts like little else. Surely, to "succeed" at love is to experience fully one of the most sublime facets of the human condition itself. How may such a feat be accomplished?

By not giving a damn about it.

But how can we plumb the depths of one of humanity's strongest emotions without giving a damn? We must address the question systematically.

⁂

What is love?

There may be as many answers to that question as men and women who have asked it over the millennia. If all the world's poets, heroes, and holy people haven't yet reached agreement on the matter, I don't suppose we will here. But there are some characteristics about which we can be confident.

⁂

Love means seeing yourself in the object of your affection

One of the most fundamental aspects of love is seeing one's own interests and concerns, in every sense, in those of the object of love, and vice versa. Love is empathy in its purest form. That sure sounds like giving a damn, doesn't it? But let's look at it more closely.

We have established that not giving a damn entails making the right choices for you in the here and now. It means living in this moment, in control of one's emotions and without undue regard for the opinions of others. It means not being trapped in the past or the future. How can these things be accomplished while seeing yourself in the object of your love?

When you fully and unreservedly locate yourself in and of the one you love, that person ceases to be an "other" for all intents and purposes. Because you don't give a damn, you make the best choices for yourself right here, right now. When you truly love another, "yourself" encompasses the object of your love. Your best choices and decisions are for him or her exactly as they are for you. Your personal reality is essentially expanded by one (or for most of us, more than one). This realization carries significant consequences. The more people you love, the wider the definition of "you" becomes. Making the right decisions for yourself in the here and now can be difficult enough; doing the same for two, three, five or more can be quite challenging.

And what happens if the best decision for you in the here and now is in conflict with the best decisions for all the other "you's" that now comprise your expanded personal identity? No one ever said making the best decision would be easy. Even in the absence of loved ones, the decision-making process always involves weighing options and considering the best of what may be several possibilities. Not giving a damn doesn't mean making a good decision—there may be a great many good decisions in any given situation—but making the best decision for you in the here and now. It requires a clear and alert mind, fully grounded in the present, to make the best decision. Mistakes are easy to make, especially if you allow outside influences to affect your decision-making process.

That having been said, making the best decisions for the "you" that includes your various loved ones need not be any more difficult than making them for you as a theoretically isolated individual. It comes down to a question of love. If you truly love someone, you will be capable (difficult) and willing (more difficult) to see yourself completely in them and vice versa. If your love is real in this sense, then choosing between two conflicting options for yourself and the one you love is no more challenging than weighing two options for yourself alone. The best decision for "you" in the here and now is the one you should take, free from fears or regrets and without subverting your reason to your emotions. If "you" includes six, seven people or more, the decision-making process may become more complex, but is essentially the same.

⁂

Love is Trust

Trust is not only essential for real love; it is an inherent aspect of it. When you locate yourself in another, you need to know without doubt that the other also finds him or herself in you—at least to a reasonable degree. That is why unrequited or false love cannot work. When you expand your understanding of self to encompass another, that other likewise expands his or her reality to include you. That is love, and it is easy to see how it relies upon trust. Both (or all) parties involved need to believe that they are part of the other just as the other is part of them. In this way, "otherness" is removed and the best decisions can be made at any moment for the expanded self that includes those who love each other. If one or both parties do not truly consider the other as the self, decisions will become unbalanced. If one party is really only making the best choices for him or herself, problems will arise sooner or later. The person making decisions just on behalf of him or herself may drag the other along for a while down a path only suited for one. The person making decisions based on a belief that he or she is part of an expanded idea of self will find those decisions out of accord with the other and must eventually recognize the imbalance or risk losing the original self altogether. Dragging someone along in your wake is the kind of selfishness we do NOT intend when we say don't give a damn, and giving someone else's damn is NOT the way to make the best decisions for you in the here and now.

The idea of love can include many kinds of relationships. Romantic love between two individuals is certainly not the only love in the world. The love that you feel for your in-laws, grandparents, cousins, children, and close friends will likely all be different from each other and certainly not the same as the love you feel for your spouse or paramour. Accordingly, locating the self in the other will be experienced differently depending upon the relationship involved. There are degrees to which one encompasses another. If the degree is not roughly mutual for both (or all) parties, then problems are likely to arise. We will explore this concept further in the next chapter. Of concern here is the fact that making decisions based on the belief that the other you see as part of yourself also sees you as part of his or herself in roughly the same degree relies heavily on trust. If you cannot be sure that this perspective is reciprocal, then you cannot be sure you are making the best decisions for the expanded notion of "you."

How can this vital trust be verified? It is a process that takes place every day in every decision that you and your loved ones make together. Not giving a damn is about each choice at each moment of the here and now. Given the nearly countless choices that we are faced with every day, it is almost certain that even the most perfectly synchronized lovers will not be in immediate agreement at all times. Even a solitary individual making choices for himself alone is forced to weigh many options in making the right choice at any given moment. Two people who see themselves in the other still represent two distinct human brains considering available options. Making the right decisions as one involves a process of negotiation and putting the interests of the expanded self above that of either of the individuals therein. In order to be willing and able to make decisions on behalf of this larger self, each individual involved must trust that the other will do likewise. Without this trust, each party will harbor insecurity about making decisions on behalf of the larger self. Distrust can lead to contracting back to making choices solely for the individual self, or falling into the imbalance mentioned previously. Not giving a damn can be tricky when more than one individual is involved as in love, but without trust it is just about impossible.

⁂

Love is Commitment

Love is a process that requires commitment. Trust is not a fleeting recognition that another locates their self in you as you do in them, but a confidence in such reciprocity built over time. As we have seen, exercising trust in a loving relationship requires negotiation and joint decision-making. Trust is consolidated as the expanded 'self' grows more adept at making decisions and not giving a damn together. This process, over time, is commitment. We have said many times that not giving a damn is all about making the best decisions for you in the here and now. How can this focus on the present rely on something that takes place over time? The answer lies in the accumulation of moments. Some people say that love is forever. It's not. Love is for right now. Put enough right nows together and you can build forever. That is commitment and that is love.

Commitment, as described above, is a process rather than a condition or declaration. Commitment is proven in every instance where the expanded self makes the best decision and doesn't give a damn about anything else. Proclaiming everlasting love is not commitment, it is just words. Commitment is found in every best decision in every here and now for the self-composed of all members who truly love one another. Commitment is the exercise, over time, of trust. Trust is the confidence that the one you see yourself in also sees their own self in you. This is love, and when you have it you don't need to give a damn about anything else.

Alas, though love is a uniquely wonderful thing, there is no guarantee that it will last any more than other wonderful things do. Love can end for any number of reasons. If any one of the three pillars of love described above fails, the entire edifice is likely to come tumbling down. If one or several parties becomes unable to commit to a relationship (and it only takes a moment) then trust begins to break down. If there is no trust then it becomes difficult to locate the self in the other. Without this, there is no love. People can change over time.

They can develop or reveal characteristics that make it impractical for two people (or more) to coexist in a single self with enough trust and commitment to not give a damn about anything else.

Sometimes the hardest thing to do is to admit when love has gone. Once you have proven commitment to a relationship it can feel like a waste of precious time to let it go. It feels as if you've lost the entire principle on an extremely important investment. Once you have given and received trust it can be a blow to the ego to admit that trust can no longer be maintained. Once you have placed your very sense of self into another, excising fully half (or more) of who you are cannot help but create a strong sense of loss. Nonetheless, if the three pillars of love are not intact it is only a matter of time before structural failure occurs. The longer you wait to get out of a collapsing building the more likely you are to be seriously hurt. This is where not giving a damn is very important.

Not giving a damn means putting yourself first and making the best choices for you at every moment. When a clear-headed, rational assessment of circumstances indicates that all the essential elements of love are no longer there, you need to fall back to your original position and start making decisions on your own behalf. Strong emotions are sure to be involved, and this is where your established habit of keeping them under control and in their proper place will pay off. At such a time, it is most important to not give a damn. If you hesitate to make what you know is the best decision for yourself in the here and now because you are worried about what your family or community will think of your "failure," or if your pride simply won't let you admit to having lost something, then you are definitely giving a damn, and negative consequences are likely to follow. Recognizing when love has gone is an important consideration and no one is likely to take it lightly, but you'll be surprised at how much easier 'difficult' decisions are when you don't give a damn.

When love has been lost it hurts. It's supposed to. The good news is that when you don't give a damn you are prepared to recognize and accept love when it comes your way again. When you refuse to be trapped by the past you won't dwell on love lost, and will be able to embrace love again at any moment. If you refuse to be trapped by the future you won't allow anxiety or expectation about what will or will not happen tomorrow to prevent you from accepting love today. If you don't give a damn about love you will always be ready to love fully and well.

CHAPTER 7

DON'T GIVE A DAMN ABOUT FAMILY

Don't give a damn about your family. Of all the admittedly formulaic statements I've filled this book with that one has to be the most difficult and disturbing to write. It sounds terrible. Of course people give a damn about their own families, right? However, considering what you certainly know by now about not giving a damn it shouldn't be too hard to consider an explanation.

Not giving a damn means, among other things, putting yourself first. But that does not mean being selfish, irresponsible, or callous; quite the contrary in fact. You cannot be useful to those who are important to you if you don't put yourself first. If you've ever actually listened to those instructions they give when you board an airplane you'll know that in the event of an emergency, if oxygen masks are deployed, you should adjust your own mask before helping children or others in need seated next to you.

Consider why this advice is given. It is the same with many things in life. If you do not put yourself first you will not be capable of doing for others. If you have family and others who rely on you, it is imperative that you put yourself first—for their sake as well as yours. Those family members, in turn, must put themselves first for your sake as well as their own. In this way, a family unit of rational and capable people can strengthen and support each other and the society in which they live. On a certain level, not giving a damn is a civic duty, as we will explore at another time.

Not giving a damn also involves not giving undue consideration to what other people think. You cannot make the best decisions for you in the present moment if you are distracted by the largely irrelevant concerns of others. Only you are in the best position to determine what is the best decision for you in the here and now (absent some disabling factor), and only you will ultimately be held most responsible for the consequences of your choices. To grant others an unwarranted place in your decision making process is to invite distraction at the least and disaster at the worst. That is not to say that there is no place for good advice and wise counsel in your life, but the bottom line must be clear; only you can make the best decisions for you right here, right now.

⁂

Who are you?

The aforementioned must be reconciled with a notion raised in an earlier chapter. The idea of "you" can be considered in a larger sense than it is usually taken. When we speak of family we are generally speaking of "loved ones" to one extent or another. Love is obviously not restricted to the man or woman (or the several combinations possible therein) with whom you may be physically intimate. You may experience love in different manners and degrees with different members of your family. Family can include parents, siblings, children, cousins, etc., in addition to spouses and lovers. To the extent that you truly love any of the above, they are essentially an extension of "you" as concerns your decision-making process. Think of "you" as a spectrum along which loved ones are displayed as closer and further from you. Anyone on the spectrum is obviously someone important to you, but those closest to you are the ones who you see as you see yourself in the decision-making process. They in turn will see you the same way provided the love involved is reciprocal in type and degree. Whereas a spouse or your offspring may be directly on top of you on the spectrum, a cousin may be found somewhere along the margin depending on your personal family situation. When we speak of not giving undue consideration to what other people think, it is in light of this type of relativity. "Others" will be those not found on your spectrum, and "you" will be all those who are, with particular identification with those closest to the center.

⁂

Children

For many people, their children would be found at some point in their lives very close if not in the exact same location as themselves on the spectrum of "you." This is especially true of young children. The younger children are the more heavily they depend on their parents/caregivers to make their decisions for them. This is why many people feel the burden of responsibility for children most heavily when those children are in a helpless condition. A baby makes almost no decisions for him or herself. An adult child, on the other hand, may move far away from his or her parents and/or become estranged from them to the point where they are only distantly located on the spectrum. The famous difficulty in dealing with teenaged children is due to the fact that they occupy an ill-defined middle ground between need and independence. During this transition, position on the spectrum may fluctuate for both parents and children, with neither sure how to relate to such changes. Throw in such variables as step children or those separated from one or both parents due to geography or circumstance and the whole thing starts to look pretty complicated.

⁂

Independence

In societies such as the United States, where independence is valued as a strong virtue in and of itself, "good" parents encourage their children to become independent as early and in as many ways as possible. This can have both positive and negative consequences. The willingness and ability to be independent is one factor that can enable children to rise above their parents' station through hard work, talent, and successful risk-taking. Older parents are able, once their children are grown, to seek their own fulfillment as individuals rather than only existing in relation to their children forever. On the other hand, there are millions and millions of Americans in senior care centers clinging to their own dwindling independence (and dignity) while their adult children pursue independent and distant lives. There are also many young adults who find that if they are not so successful risk takers they have no one to catch them when they fall. There is a cost and benefit to everything and families must adjust their relations to one another according to their values and expectations.

Brothers and sisters

Siblings are said to have some of the most important relationships in each other's lives due to the overall length of said relationships and the fact that they encompass in most cases the most influential and formative years. Nevertheless, in most families siblings would not occupy the same place on the spectrum as spouses or children. It would be an unusually close family where a brother or sister could be found in almost the same point on the spectrum as the self. This may be because each sibling is involved in the process of branching out from the central family tree in their own direction. As new families are begun, people feel the heaviest responsibility toward the extended "self" that involves those most dependent upon them. This may include spouses and children, but rarely brothers and sisters. This reality actually represents an opportunity for unique relationships between brothers and sisters, but only if such relationships are carefully cultivated and maintained.

⁂

Extended family

Somewhere on the outer edges of the spectrum of "oneself" may be found family members such as in-laws and the extended family of grandparents, cousins, etc. For some, family members of this level would not even make the scale. A source of potential conflict exists in that so many just barely do. The interests of those distant on the spectrum are less likely to be in accord and therefore more likely to clash, while at the same time each will see the other as less a part of the self. In the case of cousins and other more distant relatives this is unlikely to be much of an issue as these family members may only come into contact only rarely. However, in the case of in-laws things can get a bit trickier because someone distant on your spectrum may identify closely with your spouse who is extremely close on the same spectrum. Complex issues of identity and influence often ensue. Managing such relationships takes special care, but if you don't give a damn, the final word always rests with you.

CHAPTER 8

DON'T GIVE A DAMN ABOUT RELIGION

Faith. They say it can move mountains. Although it need not necessarily be so, the general human inclination to faith (of some, or any, sort) has tended throughout history to coalesce into religions with distinct doctrines, practices, enunciated beliefs, prohibitions, and obligations. It is generally the case that long-established religions reflect cultural traits of a given time and place that became concretized as representative of the religion in question, involve hermeneutics that include earlier influences (often from older religious traditions) and a theology that grows more complex over time until it achieves a relatively standard, reproducible form that specialists may assist lay people in interpreting and applying to a variety of changing social, cultural, and historical conditions. Such experts may also, from time to time, be called upon to reconcile the tenets of a given religion with changes in knowledge of history, our physical world, and/or accepted scientific notions. Because humans are most essentially social beings, organized religions have tended to develop as functions of community. When this tendency combines with typical human fears and weaknesses, it is not surprising that religions have so often become the vehicles for tribalism, separation, and even war. Faith and religion seem like things that a great many people give a damn about, but it doesn't have to be that way. Faith applies very appropriately to not giving a damn, and religion can as well.

⁎ ⁎ ⁎

Faith and giving a damn

The notion of faith is almost perfectly suited to not giving a damn. By definition, faith involves believing in something that cannot be proven. When you think about it, this means that every human being who has ever lived has and does rely on faith to one degree or another. Perhaps the inescapable necessity of faith in the life of limited creatures like humans is why it has always played such a prominent role in human affairs. Our earliest ancestors required a primitive faith in order to function and survive in a world that demonstrated—through the occasional natural disaster, climate change, or solar eclipse—that it always contained a degree of unpredictability. Throughout recorded history notions about life, health, and the physical world that were almost universally accepted as "true" and immutable by the people of a given period have always been dispelled eventually by new discoveries or creative insights. Rather than destroy our willingness to embrace absolutes, such changes have consistently resulted in a transference of our faith into a new set of "truths." If people gave too much of a damn we would never get over the shattering of what was once firmly believed to be true, and adaptation to a new "reality" would not take place.

⁂

Faith and humanity

What makes us human requires faith from us, however it may be manifested. Abstract thinking, the basis of higher human intelligence, relies upon a kind of faith. Abstract thinking demonstrates the ability to apply knowledge from one set of circumstances to another is indicative of abstract thinking. When archaeologists first discovered evidence of burial ceremonies among primitive humans they knew that they had hit upon proof of higher thinking in our ancestors. Being able to imagine that their dead might have use of the tools and decorations used during their lives after they had apparently moved on to a different reality showed abstract thinking at work. Now, decorating a dead man before throwing dirt over him might not seem so impressive today, but it expresses an important aspect of human cognition: faith.

⁂

Faith from the beginning

Consider the life of our ancient forebear. His very existence would depend upon recognizing and recalling patterns in the world around him. See an animal that tends to kill humans: better remember that. The distinction between nutritious and poisonous fruit: good to note. The migration patterns of your prey animals and seasonal grains: very important. Here the ancient "scientist" was highly valuable. But no matter how often the observed truths were relayed via oral tradition, sooner or later some disaster or climate shift, or population change would destroy everything our ancestors were trying to live by. They would have to be flexible and they would have to adjust the faith that gave order to their lives as circumstances dictated. This "flexible faith" allowed our distant cousins to order their daily existence and adjust to changing circumstances and "reality."

We are little changed today. Our lives; our personal life, our professional life, our understanding of one another and the physical world, are always changing. Of necessity we try to find patterns and build routines to order our lives, but just like our cavemen kin we are knocked off our pins every time an act of nature overturns our expectations and puts the lie to our confidence.

The bottom line is that we must believe what we cannot know for sure in order to function on this highly volatile rock we occupy. This, as much as anything, is the basis of all kinds of faith. Our caveman could have cowered all day behind a rock but he never would have killed a Mammoth that way. Magellan could have turned back long before getting to the Philippines but circumnavigation wouldn't have happened at that time. We were never absolutely required to strap human beings to the top of giant bullets and shoot them into space but we wouldn't have landed on the Moon otherwise. We have an insatiable need to expand our limits, and we could never do so without a sense of faith.

This may all seem a bit extreme, but the same faith that motivated all the aforementioned lays at the heart of our major faith traditions today. I may not subscribe to any of these particular traditions or belief systems but I recognize that faith itself is a key component of human intelligence. An inconsistent and unreliable one but a key nonetheless. Naturally, an animal as aggressive and violent as the human would turn something as universal and uniting as this into an excuse for killing, dividing, and oppressing and that is just what has happened over the millennia.

⌘ ⌘ ⌘

Uniting principle

Considering that all faith carries at its core the same fundamental cognition it would seem that the relatively minor details distinguishing each manifestation would not be as extreme as our reactions to them have suggested throughout history. As a matter that cannot be proven or disproved, faith should be something that we accept in one another without angst. If a physical property can be proven or disproved then there is cause for attention to veracity, but when the topic is a question of faith then arguing is obviously going to get us nowhere.

When you believe something that cannot concretely be demonstrated one way or another based on your personal faith why on earth would you give a damn what someone else thinks? Faith for what it is loses its purpose if there is no mystery or uncertainty to it. Yes, people of great faith claim to have no doubt, but the entire point is that faith must contain an element of doubt. This is the point that escapes the unthinking adherent and the militant atheist alike. The human capacity to believe is what is most important here.

If you believe in something that cannot be proven or disproved, what is the only reasonable reaction to a questioning of your belief (or disbelief)? That's right: don't give a damn.

As manifestations of the human capacity (and compulsion) for faith, all of the world's major religions present insights into the human psyche and how we relate to the world, each other, and the inescapable realities of human existence. I cannot claim to be an adherent of any particular religion, but I recognize that there is a comfort and a kind of strength to be found within them.

⁂

Judaism

I certainly can't claim to be Jewish, but those folks have a few good ideas. Like many organized religions, one of the strengths of Judaism is its sense of community. There are many types and interpretations of Judaism, but generally speaking all Jews recognize one another as members of a community of faith wherever they may be. In other words, all Jews are members of a global family. Recall what we have said previously about family and not giving a damn. Close family members and other loved ones are, for all intents and purposes, extensions of the "you" for whom you make all decisions in the here and now. The closer a family member is to your original self the more completely their interests and yours converge in considering what is best for you at any given moment. A community of faith functions in a very similar manner.

The fact that Judaism represents a family of faith can be a good in and of itself in several ways. A real sense of community is one of the more reliable ways of promoting harmony among members of said community. One of the sources of the unfortunately frequent incidences of crime in modern urban settings is the sense of isolation and alienation that has accompanied the growth of the mega-metropolises so much of humanity inhabits today. If you cannot see yourself in the other—any other—there is very little incentive to follow another of Judaism's precepts: do unto others as you would have them do unto you. If you remember the basic qualities of love we discussed earlier, you will know that empathy is essential to experiencing this most noble of human interactions. Certainly, love and community may be achieved without organized re-ligion, but any faith that fosters such positive factors has something to recommend it.

✖ ✖ ✖

Christianity

I certainly can't claim to be Christian, but those folks have a few good ideas. Like Judaism, Christianity contains the essential elements of community and love. In fact, the idea of love is central to Christianity. The Christian admonition to love thy neighbor as you love thyself is reminiscent of the older faith from which it diverged. Christianity takes the concept of seeing the self in the other to metaphoric and metaphysical heights in the mystery of the Trinity and the ritual of the Eucharist. Through these theological devices, seeing the self in the other reaches potentially universal dimensions. For Christians, Christ literally sees himself in God, and followers are encouraged to see themselves in Christ in so far as they are called upon to follow in his footsteps and continue his work. It's difficult to imagine a more comprehensive religious expression of love than this degree of expansion of the self.

In addition to this foundational principle of love through faith, Christianity also matches well with the idea of not giving a damn in its emphasis on the forgiveness of sins. What could fit the concept of not giving a damn better than admitting to mistakes, apologizing for them, and then moving on without becoming trapped by regret or worry. If you sincerely admit to your sins and take steps to atone for them, Christians are taught, you are assured of a positive response from a forgiving God. It seems that Christ wants his followers to stop giving a damn and get back to doing his work.

Islam

I certainly can't claim to be Muslim, but those folks have a few good ideas. Like Judaism and Christianity, Islam evokes a sense of community and the expression of love through empathy. The teachings of Islam clearly state that if you don't love for your brother what you love for yourself, you aren't getting the idea. Another aspect of love that we discussed earlier is that of commitment, and Islam certainly does encourage commitment in its adherents. It should come as no surprise that these three closely related faiths should share basic theological underpinnings to a significant degree. Where they have historically dropped the ball is in giving entirely too much of a damn about each other as distinct faiths.

⁂

Buddhism

I certainly can't claim to be Buddhist, but those folks have a few good ideas. The Buddhist rejection of material goods as objects of and conduits to desire fits well our notion of not giving a damn. If you refer to the chapter on not giving a damn about money, you will see how de-emphasizing the worth of material goods could aid in the making of right decisions about lifestyle and the use of limited resources. Many of our materialist cultures today could benefit from a dose of Buddhism in this regard.

The Buddhist goal of destroying the ego also fits our theme nicely. In so many cases, it is the unrestrained ego that leads to distraction, traps, and poor choices. Actually killing the ego may be an unrealistic thing for all but the most adept to accomplish, but a properly tamed ego surely makes not giving a damn a lot easier.

Taoism

I certainly can't claim to be Taoist, but those folks have a few good ideas. In fact, Taoism is one of the religions best suited to not giving a damn. In simplest terms, it involves just following the natural way of the universe as most appropriate for each being in each circumstance. This means doing what is manifestly most obvious and natural in every moment, following paths of least resistance and not attempting to do or be what is against the character of each creature and condition. That sounds a lot like not giving a damn to me.

Theologians and adherents to any of the faiths referred to above may object to my admittedly simplistic treatment of these traditions but the point holds that faith and religion, for all the fervor, angst, and even bloodshed that have been expended in their names over the millennia, can coincide with not giving a damn. In its most sublime incarnation, faith can expand the sense of seeing yourself in the other to encompass all of humanity. This is a lofty spiritual goal that eludes most of us, including especially those of us with a rather underdeveloped facility with faith, but in the end it all leads back to the same basic premise with which we began. Even seeing all things as "you" recommends making right choices and doing what is best for you right here right now. In other words, not giving a damn.

CHAPTER 9

DON'T GIVE A DAMN ABOUT TECHNOLOGY

One of the distinguishing characteristics of our species has always been our uniquely sophisticated ability to make and use tools. We've come a long way from spears and primitive stone blades to the iPad 2 (or whatever else by the time you're reading this). Of course being what we are, humans have always found inventive ways and reasons to use our natural abilities to harm one another. So it has always been with technology. Our own greatest natural advantage is also our greatest threat to ourselves. The more that our ability to exploit this gift has grown, the more potential hazards and com-plications have been introduced into our lives.

With the passage of time the pace of technological innovation has only increased; each advancement laying the foundation for many more to follow. A time traveler from one hundred years ago would find our world more unfathomable than a similar traveler from one thousand years before his. And who knows what our own near future holds? So it is that never before have we been less prepared to keep up with our own tools. It is all too easy to become swamped or enslaved by technology rather than remaining the master of it. The best way to keep it in its place is to not give a damn.

⁂

Why technology

Technology can make our lives easier, our work more efficient and productive, and our leisure time more stimulating. Instant communication and access to nearly unlimited information about almost anything marks a revolutionary change that many of us take for granted despite the fact that this new reality is still a relatively recent development. Some may say that this indicates an inherent ability in humans to adapt to such technological changes, but that would only be fooling ourselves. We try to adapt, to make any new reality seem "normal," but that's exactly where we can get lost. We allow ourselves to get swept up into new structures of communication and expectation, but too often do so with-out considering what we are doing and why. Next thing you know, we have hundreds of "friends" and thousands of "followers" in the real/unreal universe of social media, and spend an alarming percentage of our day texting or tweeting or updating; sacrificing time and energy that could certainly be devoted to more productive pursuits. Try to calculate how much time you have spent in the past 12 months following tangents of information on the internet unrelated to what you originally logged on to find. For many of us, the answer is shocking. For all the benefits that modern technology has given us in terms of communication and information, it has also provided us with novel and attractive ways to lose ourselves. Not giving a damn is all about looking out for yourself.

⁂

Unavoidable

The practical reality of the world most of us live in is that the pervasiveness of technology is all but unavoidable to a certain extent. Most of us need to make use in our private and/or professional lives of the advanced communications and other technology available to us. The trick is to use this technology without being used by it; to be aware of and control the degree to which technology is integrated into our lives. This can be harder than it sounds, but is more important than you may have previously considered.

⁂

Take stock

Start by taking an inventory of all the equipment, machines, devices, and gadgets that you use in your daily life. Use an old fashioned pencil and paper to write it all down. You may find yourself surprised at what a long list you can generate. Next to each item on your list, take note of what it is used for. This part can be harder than it seems. Some items, like your cell phone, may be used for a great variety of things (actually using it as a phone coming in somewhere near the bottom of the list). For other items, like the television, you might have to admit that they are seldom used for anything of redeeming value. The next step is to record, as accurately as possible, how much time you spend each day interacting with each of the items on your list. For many people, adding up the total of all the times thus noted results in a number disturbingly close to every waking hour in a day. Keep this list someplace safe. It can become a worksheet for disentangling your life and giving less of a damn while not sacrificing the potential benefits of technology.

In an earlier chapter, we recommended taking some time every day to simply reflect on yourself as a living, finite being. Your "gadget list" can be used in a similar way. Take some time every now and then to review the list and consider what it says about how you are living with technology. For each item on your list, try to consciously consider the necessity of the device and the cost/benefit of the time and attention devoted to it. Be aware of how much you are using these devices and how much they are using you. Keep your conclusions in mind as you make decisions every moment of every day.

⁂

Keep technology in its place

When you have a clearer understanding of your relationship to all the "things" in your life, you will be better situated to make good choices about their use. For many of us, this will mean allowing our devices to consume far less of our time each day. A greater awareness of the role of technology in our lives will inform the choices we make every moment, with the likely result that we use less of them. The best decision regarding technology and what is important to you right now will naturally mean paring down to the real necessities. In practical terms, this means you will make the best use of technology and avoid letting it make your life more complicate, distracted and controlled (addicted). With this heightened awareness, you should see your "on" time go down and feel yourself more in control of your choices.

For some of us, our work, study, and relationships will necessitate a greater use of things like the internet, communications devices, and social media than for others even when brought back down to a practical minimum. There is nothing inherently wrong with this, but it will require a greater degree of concentration and control to avoid falling into the trap of constant connectivity. Even for those of us who cannot avoid being "wired" for a significant part of the day, it is important to set aside some "offline" time every day.

Consider it a form of meditation, rejuvenation, or deprogramming that your body and mind require in order to function at peak efficiency and make good decisions at all times.

⁂

Beware shiny things

An important consideration regarding technology is not being suckered into "needing" the latest gadget. This sounds obvious, but it can be hard to resist the lure of shiny new things. Refer to the chapter on not giving a damn about money for a detailed explanation of how and why to avoid this kind of wrongly-inspired consumerism. It's no secret that obsolescence is built into much of the technology that impacts our lives, just as there is no mystery to why the "upgraded" version of many things are rolled out on a regular schedule. It is up to you to make good choices at every moment.

✖✖✖

Positive uses

Making good choices about technology is not limited to reducing its impact on our lives. We need to make that impact a positive one. Beyond making certain that too much of our time and attention is not occupied by an invasively wired world, using technology effectively is also important. Cell phones can be very useful for all manner of personal and professional communication—even for personal safety—but causing a car accident by texting while driving clearly negates any benefit the device might bring. The internet is a vast and extremely convenient source for research and networking, but if you allow the near-infinite possibilities distract you then it becomes just another way of wasting time. For all the good that can be found online, there is a great deal of harmful content that is wise to avoid (and to keep from children, for example).

Social networking is famous for fostering shallow and superficial connections between people, or even allowing those with ill intent to harm others. However, if a social networking source can provide a real and meaningful community for a well-defined group of people of like interest, then it can be a very positive place for people to learn, interact, or even organize socially beneficial activities to take place in the real world. The crude stone tools of early humans could be used to hunt and prepare food, or to murder rivals. Since the beginning, technology has been what we make of it. Always remember that the greatest device you will ever use or need is your own mind and the ability to make the right choices for you at every moment. Don't give a damn and you will make the most of your tools.

CHAPTER 10

DON'T GIVE A DAMN ABOUT YOUR JOB

For most of us, work is an unavoidable fact of life. If we want to put food on the table and keep ourselves housed and clothed (not to mention giving the government its "share") we must work. Considering that a large portion of our lives is devoted to preparing to be able to work, looking for work, trying to keep a job, trying to advance on the job or find a better one, and relating to your prior job in retirement, it is certainly a topic of great significance to most of us. As a result, it is also considered a source of great anxiety for many. It needn't be, not if you don't give a damn.

⁂

Work as part of who you are

Work can be seen as a necessary chore, or as an integral part of your identity as a person. Some may find the latter idea shocking, but both are important to consider. We don't all manage to find a job we love, and probably none of us loves our job all the time. Nonetheless, the necessity of work is unavoidable. The condition of the labor market at any given time, as well as each individual's particular skills, experience, and education, serve to guide and often limit likely job prospects. As a result, while some manage to find work in our chosen field, quite often we are forced to "settle" for whatever work we can secure that will allow us to meet our needs and responsibilities. People working in the field for which they trained and intended are not always happy with their employment, but those who have "settled" for whatever work they can find are rarely so. This is where many people create stress in themselves by giving a damn. While it is certainly understandable that one might find such work and the circumstances that necessitate it somewhat disappointing, it is here that one must avoid the traps of the past and future that lay strewn along such a path.

⁂

Traps and work

It is difficult to do a job as well as one might when preoccupied with what it could have been rather than what it is. If the job you currently have does not make use of training and education that you at some point went out of your way to complete, then failed expectations can adversely affect motivation. This is not surprising, but also not productive. Not giving a damn means making the best decisions for you in the here and now.

Even when working at a less-than-ideal job it will likely be rare that acquitting yourself as well as possible is not the best choice at any given moment. Try to imagine the circumstances under which it would be best to demonstrate that you cannot do a job well or be counted on to complete tasks, particularly if you consider those tasks beneath you. Allowing disappointment over a divide between earlier expectations and current conditions to prevent you from doing your best can only reflect poorly on you and in the end limit future prospects. This is how the trap of the past can hobble the future. If your current position does not make use of your training, education, and experience, try to find ways to make it so while doing your very best at whatever task is in front of you right now. Even (especially) if you do not like what you are doing, performing to the best of your abilities at anything is the surest way to access future opportunities. Being distracted by concerns that your current job is not as challenging, rewarding, or enriching as prior jobs will not enhance your current situation. Indulging in feelings of regret over where you thought you would be in your professional life by now can only make it less likely that you ever do realize those higher expectations. By "proving" that you cannot do your current job well you make it less likely that you will find your way to a better one. Allowing yourself to be trapped in the past solidifies—at most—your current status and limits your likely opportunities in the future. Not giving a damn means making the best choices right now, doing your best at every given moment no matter what the job, and avoiding the traps that can limit you.

Ambition

Ambition can be a positive thing when it encourages you to make the best decisions right now in light of realistic and measured goals. However, like most useful things it can become dangerous if not properly controlled. Ambition is beneficial if it drives you to do the very best you can on whatever task is set before you right now in the expectation that good decisions and excellence in anything you do will allow positive results to accumulate and result in further opportunities. Ambition is detrimental however if it leads you to dwell on dissatisfaction with your current position to such an extent that you do not put your full attention and best effort into the task at hand, thereby diminishing future opportunities. This kind of ambition becomes a trap of the future. Planning and setting realistic goals is a good idea, but if you spend all your time looking downfield you will drop the ball every time. Future traps are self-defeating and only lead to great frustration with a situation you may be preventing yourself from growing out of. Useful ambition encourages not giving a damn because it results in the same positive behavior of making the right choices and doing your very best right now.

⁂

Dissatisfaction

No one can predict future conditions with a high degree of accuracy. Even the most consistent accumulation of good decisions does not always bring about the most positive results. You may toil for years at a job you would like to grow out of, only to find that at the crucial moment market conditions or other variables outside your control seem to conspire against your goals. Under these circumstances it is easy to fall into a pattern of negative and self-defeating thought and behavior, but it is at just such a time that it is most important not to give a damn. There will always be setbacks, sometimes big ones, but the long game is won by the steady hand. Even the most successful investors lose money in the stock market, but they are successful precisely because they don't panic and overreact to downturns. The same principle holds for someone working at a job they are not satisfied with. If a long hoped-for opportunity for advancement does not pan out, there is no reason to panic and quit your current job without having another lined up, or falling into a state of surly despair that can only make future opportunities less likely. Focusing on making the best decisions and doing your best work right now, while expanding your knowledge and education in some way every day is the way to win the long game.

⁂

Satisfaction

Not everyone is dissatisfied with their job. There are those for whom their work defines them to a significant degree. These are people whose identity is connected to their job in a positive way. Such people are in the best position to not give a damn. I'm tempted to advise us all to try to relate to our jobs this way because the benefits are so evident, but I realize that for many people various circumstances make it unlikely. Those who identify themselves, at least in part, by the work they do, naturally make work-related decisions at any given moment in relation to what is best for them both professionally and personally. Just as the concept of "you" expands to include loved ones and close family members, so too does it include the work a person does when that work is part of how a person self-identifies. If you literally see yourself in your work you will likely make decisions for and about your job that reflect how you want to perceive yourself. This makes it much less likely that you will give a damn about things unrelated or insignificant to your own best interests at any given moment.

Of course there are still dangers to be avoided even in such a positive scenario. These involve the risk of emotional overreach and how that can lead to traps of the future. A positive outlook on one's job can lead to over-exuberance that not infrequently results in unrestrained ego. Make no mistake, this can be as hazardous as frustration and regret in diverting attention away from making the right decisions right now. An over-active ego can lead to taking on too much or over estimating your true abilities. Both can have unfortunate consequences. It should also be remembered that no matter how much you may like your job, or how strongly you identify yourself thereby, it is still just your job. Identifying too strongly can lead to giving very much of a damn and losing sight of all the other important aspects of your life. Even positive emotions can distract you from the right choices if you allow them to control you rather than vice versa.

HR people frequently speak of "job satisfaction." The most positive and useful satisfaction you can get from your job is to not give a damn about it. Spending time and energy worrying about whether or not you are satisfied with your job can only distract you from focusing on the here and now. As with all the topics discussed here, accumulating a series of good choices and right decisions will inevitably result in positive things. If you are satisfied with your job it hardly seems necessary to constantly remind yourself of the fact instead of concentrating on the job itself. Excessive self-indulgence can result from undue concern with your own satisfaction. This can lead easily to the traps of the future we discussed previously. Concern over dissatisfaction with your job can lead to frustration and traps of the past. Certainly, if you are dissatisfied with your job you can be expected to take steps to improve your situation and/or find another position, but when faced with a given task to complete the most effective way to approach it is to simply focus on mak-ing the best decisions and doing your best work right now. Don't give a damn about whether or not you are satisfied; just complete each task to the best of your ability as they arise. You may be surprised at how quickly the effects of excessive satisfaction or dissatisfaction are mitigated in this way, and what opportunities open up for you.

⁂

Work as image

It can be a very positive thing to identify yourself with the work you do, but too many people take this in the wrong direction and start to consider their job part of an "image" of themselves they want to portray to the rest of the world. Needless to say, this is quite the opposite of not giving a damn. People for whom their job is part of an "image" are wrongly motivated, and frequently make decisions that have unproductive consequences. Seeing a job as part of an image one wishes to project can lead one to take or pursue a job for the wrong reasons. This often results in frustration at being unable to secure a job for which one may be unqualified or otherwise unsuited. It can also result in finding oneself in over one's head at a job, or ultimately unsatisfied with the reality of the actual work behind the image. Concern with the image of a job can lead to future traps where ambition is placed ahead of competence and a position or promotion becomes the focus of attention rather than doing each task as well as possible in the present. Worrying about image means giving a damn about what other people—people who in all likelihood couldn't really care less about you—think instead of doing what is best for you at every given moment. All honest work is honorable, and any job that fulfills your needs is satisfactory. What other people think should be the last thing you care about.

Insecurity

It's not always easy to find or keep a job. Given the state of the economy at any given time, you may find yourself without a job. This can be a difficult situation, and one that leads many people into traps or to allow their emotions to get the upper hand. It is just the time when you need to not give a damn. Searching for a job can be frustrating and demoralizing if you let it be. For many people the ego has a hard time accepting the label "unemployed." The term can feel like a synonym for "inferior," "unqualified," or "unwanted." These are not adjectives people readily embrace. However, such terms only carry any weight at all to the extent that we are concerned with how others perceive us. If you really don't give a damn you can direct all the energy you would have used worrying about such things to the matter at hand.

Directing your job search calmly and realistically, attempting to shut out irrelevant influences and make the best decisions in every moment, will move you toward your goal much faster than agonizing over what it says about you that you are between jobs. Not giving a damn also means making use of whatever resources you can as needed. If filing for unemployment feels like a blow to your pride, then you have let pride exert too much influence on your thought processes. There is danger in letting emotions such as pride affect your decision-making. See the chapter on not giving a damn about money for related issues.

Succumbing to despair and defeatism is also a mistake. This is the opposite side of letting your ego to run rough-shod over you. Giving up on looking for work and settling into a "comfortable" permanency with what should be considered temporary measures is also an indication that you are allowing emotions to play too large a role in addressing the choices you make at every moment. It can feel "easy" to fall into such a condition, but the consequences are anything but easy. Searching for a job should be approached the way as actually doing a job. Without undue concern over what has come before or what you expect to come next, the task at hand should be taken as it is and addressed by doing your best and mak-ing right decisions right now. Falling prey to traps and out-of-control emotions can only make success less likely and longer in coming. Not giving a damn will likely get you there before you know it.

⁂

Retirement

Part of working also involves saving and preparing to retire. This is also best addressed by not giving a damn. Saving for retirement is facilitated by all that we have said thus far about making responsible, realistic, clear-headed financial decisions at every step along the way, and not concerning yourself with such irrelevancies as "image." Retirement should come as the culmination of a great many right decisions over a period of years or decades. If you haven't given a damn, you should be reasonably prepared when the time comes. But if you come to "retirement age" and find you are not yet there, just put your head back down and keep working—keep making good choices—for as long as it takes, without letting outside concerns distract you. And if in retirement you find you have a hard time thinking of yourself as a person "without" a job, then you let identification with work take too deep a hold. Don't worry; it is never too late to not give a damn.

CHAPTER 11

HOW I HAVE NOT GIVEN A DAMN

As I mentioned at the outset of this book, I used to give a damn about a lot of things. I was as consumed by my own personal fears, ambitions, and emotions as anyone. Like so many of us, I had internalized the idea that passion was a sign of determination and commitment and that if I just wanted something bad enough, and exerted enough energy no matter how undirected, that I would by sheer force of will alter reality and achieve whatever my heart desired. The more difficult or frustrating things became, the more I would (literally) clench my teeth and frantically pump out energy and emotion as if by demonstrating to the world and myself how much I really, really wanted something I would therefore deserve it and the universe would acquiesce to my wishes. Needless to say, this approach was both exhausting and often disappointing. It took a long time for me to finally recognize something important. At those times in my life, whatever the circumstances, that I just didn't give a damn—out of resignation or fatigue—I felt much better and things tended to work out more favorably more often. Over many years and through a great deal of failure and success I finally worked out what it means to not give a damn and how it could affect my life and the lives of those I consider a part of myself. Once I had worked this out to my own satisfaction, I began applying the concept more deliberately to all areas of my life. I have been gratified with the results so far. It's been a long road to get to where I am in life now, and as long as I don't give a damn I'm reasonably confident that there are more positive things to come.

As I've said, when I was a young man I certainly gave a damn about a lot of things. Reflecting upon my life from the perspective of many decades I can see more clearly things that were all but a blur of emotion and un-harnessed energy in my youth. Considering who and what I was in those earlier years I sometimes wonder if it would even have been possible for me not to have given a damn back then. Young people are, as if by design, fairly brimming with power and vitality. All this energy is not tempered or directed by experience and so we have all the familiar consequences of youthful indiscretion and recklessness. However, I do believe, my own experience notwithstanding, that young people are capable of not giving a damn as well. There's no telling what a young person with a clear mind and a calm heart as well as all that energy might accomplish. This is where family and love come into play.

The bonds of family are not merely quaint tradition, but one kind of survival mechanism that human beings have, from time to time and place to place, relied upon for the mutual support of a number of people connected by blood or other ties. We have seen how, when love is truly present, the concept of oneself takes on greater dimensions than just a solitary individual. Family is a recognition of the bonds that create and maintain this larger concept of oneself. Where love expands the idea of "one" to include more than just a single individual, making the best decisions for oneself in the here and now takes into consideration the reality of all constituents. In a family, this usually includes components from different age groups. This is how the experience and perspective of age can direct and focus the energies of youth. For all the ways in which a multi-faceted concept of "one" complicates the decision-making process, here we can see its potential benefit. Of course this only works when there is a sufficiently diverse yet concrete unit within which a mutually beneficial balance of interests and abilities can affect the decision-making process in a positive way.

Unfortunately, in many societies today such units are missing, fractured, or rejected. The result is too many people giving too much of a damn about too many things, with predictably unfortunate results. One only needs to glance at the local, national, or international news on any given day to see what I mean. More than that, one need only glance around oneself with all this in mind to realize the practical effects of all we have been discussing here. In the following, I offer my own story as an example of all the aforementioned. While neither as extreme nor benign as some cases, I believe my tale is in many ways representative nonetheless.

The United States is a nation of immigrants. I should know, as I am one myself. I was brought to the US by my mother when I was 12 years old. Even at such a young age I gave a damn about a lot of things. Having suffered physical and mental abuse in my native South Korea, I was a fearful and anxious child. Being thrown into a completely alien social and linguistic environment only exacerbated my insecurities and locked me into traps from which it would take many years to escape. A degree of uncertainty is to be expected in the emotional development of a child, and it is here where the love and support of a family can act as a mitigating factor. Unfortunately I, like many others, did not enjoy such support. My mother struggled with her own traps as well as the insistent demands of struggling to survive within the very jaws of poverty. To the extent that there ever was a father figure present, it was only a source of fear, violence, or resentment. Over time we drew to ourselves, as if by gravitational force, some of the extended family that would have been the norm back in our native country, but this only amounted to an extenuation of the negative influences I was unprepared to keep at bay.

Many people have personal stories of being "the new kid" at school, and how nervous and self-conscious it made them feel. Well, as one of only a very, very few Koreans in Midwestern USA at the time, I was "the new kid" to a certain degree all through junior and senior high school. I gave a damn, and wasted a lot of energy because of it. I gave a damn about not being a native English speaker and how that affected my interactions with almost everyone around me. I gave a damn about the cheap, used, or homemade clothes I wore and all the little social and cultural nuances that I didn't take for granted like my fellow students. If I could get back half the energy I spent worrying over such things I could probably cure cancer, build a perpetual-motion machine, and master interstellar travel in a weekend! It's rarely easy to navigate the process of physical, mental, and emotional maturation and for immigrants it can be even harder, but not having a source of balance somewhere else in my life made it that much more difficult. I struggled with traps of the past, present, and future for a long time.

Years later, when I had learned to not give a damn, I began to look at my own immigrant experience in a different light. I recognize all the obstacles I had to overcome, but I see them now as opportunities that I might have made more of if I didn't give a damn. Still, I can't be too hard on my younger self, as he had to work all this out more or less on his own. The past is past and while I acknowledge that the rocky paths I've walked have all led me to where I am now, my concern today is with this moment and the choices in front of me right now. I am and consider myself an American and I am mindful of all the opportunities available to me here and now that my country makes possible.

As a young boy in South Korea I had been impressed by the US military, whose presence there at the time was hard not to notice. Ever since, I harbored a desire to wear the uniform and be part of something I saw as strong, determined, and united. Perhaps it represented an order, support, and certainty that was lacking in my life. Or maybe as a little boy I just liked the hats. For whatever reason, after what was undoubtedly a less than efficient expenditure of energy, I managed to be accepted to the US Naval Academy. I did and still do consider this a significant accomplishment in my life. Although life at the academy wasn't exactly easy on minorities, it wasn't easy on anyone, especially in the first year, and I was as impressed with the institution and the education I received there as I had expected to be.

It was during the summer following that first year that I experienced what I believe was my first important instance of not giving a damn. I spent part of that summer back in South Korea visiting family and doing what young men do. It was there I met a certain young woman and quickly fell in love. I was faced with an immediate and rather stark decision to make. I was proud of what I had achieved at the academy and knew that further opportunities would open up as I advanced there, but I felt that I had found something unique with this young woman. I knew that if I tried to conduct a long-distance relationship, her family would have made "arrangements" for her before I finished at the academy. I had to make a choice right then and there. Strong arguments presented themselves on both sides, and of course many people had many opinions to offer. Some people in her family and mine felt, not unreasonably, that we were going too fast. My best friend at the academy urged me to stay on there, and a senior commander who I had always found harsh and intimidating expressed—in his own way—genuine concern not only for my future career but for my personal well-being. It is something that I have never forgotten. All I could do was to look at the choices in front of me clearly and honestly and make the best decision for me without concern for the conflicting opinions of others. The situation required me to not give a damn and just make a choice.

As an early effort at not giving a damn I can wonder just how clearly I was thinking and how successful at keeping emotions (and hormones) out of the process I was, but in any case it stands as a watershed moment for me. The consequences of my ultimate decision to drop out of the academy and marry the young woman could be presented both for and against the choice I made, but it was nevertheless an important step in my evolving world view. Before I learned to master the stubbornly insistent feeling known as regret I would agonize from time to time over my decision, but the fact of the matter is that the ten years I spent married to my first wife are part of the process by which I became the person I am today. The young man I was then made his choice and there is no point in me second-guessing him now. I am who I am today and only the choices in front of me now need concern me. I learned a lot from my many experiences during those years and recognize the value of the love we shared, but the past is past.

Once I had separated from the Naval Academy I was forced to consider the next step in my education and what kind of career I would pursue. Despite being young, married, and poor I determined to pursue a career in medicine. There were some very lean years as my wife and I both grappled with academics and basic survival. When my undergraduate education was complete, I applied to a number of medical schools. I exerted the same kind of frantic, tooth-grindingly determined energy that I had always associated with "working hard" as I prepared for and applied to these schools. When, despite my most urgent and heart-felt efforts I was not accepted at my first choice I was fairly devastated. I struggled with the feeling that I had failed, and this preoccupation followed me to the medical school where I was accepted and completed my basic education in medicine. My studies there suffered from my unsettled feelings and distracted concerns of the past and future. I was fortunate enough to receive some good advice from a professor I respected, but it was not until I personally decided to set aside distractions and focus on what I was doing that I was able to show what I was capable of. It would be a long time before I fully appreciated how much my future career rested upon the ability to not give a damn about the school that rejected me and concentrate on what was right in front of me.

You have no doubt noticed that I used the term "first wife" and realize that it implies a second. Indeed there came a time after nearly ten years when I recognized that my relationship with my first wife had changed. For some time I didn't want to accept what this might mean. I looked at the failed examples of marriage given by my mother and father and didn't want to be saddled with what I thought was shame. Both my mother and father had made messes of a number of relationships and I was trapped in their past. I was also trapped in the future as I fretted over what might come next in my life if our marriage ended. It was only when I looked clearly at the present that I came to the conclusion that the best choice for me (and her, as I still loved her in a way) was to end the marriage. It was a difficult decision but when I looked at things without giving a damn I could come to no other conclusion. I do believe, considering how things turned out for both of us, that it was the right one. Regardless, it is now unalterably in the past.

It turns out, despite what I had

feared at the time that the end of one relationship does not mean the end of the capacity for love. Quite the contrary. With the end of my first marriage I found myself with an excess capacity for love that had perhaps been building for some time. My path crossed that of a woman with similar interests, career goals, and unmet emotional needs and in due time we were wed. This marriage too lasted about ten years, but also involved children. My sense of "oneself" expanded more than it ever had before. The responsibility of being a father helped to sharpen the sense of not giving a damn that I was gradually becoming more aware of. When your choices are more or less for you alone, it is easier to become distracted by emotions or selfish desires. When "you" involves others, you must look at things clearly and rationally and this lends itself to not giving a damn.

Who would not make what they thought was the right choice for their children just because they were concerned about what the next door neighbor might think? It seems ridiculous, but in many and subtle ways many people do think this way, perhaps without even being aware of it. One danger hidden in the responsibility of parenthood is thinking that making a decision that is not good for you somehow shows how much you care about your children. The fact is that a decision that harms you in some way can only be detrimental to those who rely on you. This applies to the work you do, the food you eat, the activities you engage in and the goals you set. It would be foolish to think that cutting off your own head will make your body stronger. It is just as foolish to think that making a decision that harms yourself in some way will make your family stronger or your loved ones better off (life insurance fraud aside).

The fact that my sense of "oneself" had expanded to include my children as well as my wife made it all the more difficult when my second marriage came to an end. I struggled with this decision even more than that of my first marriage because my children were involved. However, it had become clear that the paths and interests that had converged were moving inevitably in different directions. The feelings that had been there at the outset had cooled on her part and sought different outlet on mine. It is not an unusual story, but I was faced with a difficult decision because of my expanded sense of self. For a time I thought that I simply must endure for the sake of the children, but eventually saw that I couldn't be making the best decision for them by making the wrong one for me and my wife. Weighing all of "my" interests was not easy, but when I sat myself down and deliberately looked at the situation without giving a damn the choice was clear. This time I didn't care what anyone else might think or how it might look. My only concern was with what was the right choice for me (the expanded "me"). I realized that ending my second marriage might make me look callous, irresponsible, or fickle, but I couldn't give a damn about that. I couldn't help making a mental note of the example of my own parents—my father in particular—but I set it aside as immaterial to the choice in front of me at the time. An essential part of making this decision was carefully planning how the interests of the children would be seen to and how they would remain a central part of my life and that of my second wife. Although the marriage ended, my expanded sense of self could never contract past my children.

Time and human nature being what they are, I did find love again. Now, at the age of 50, I am the proud father of two-year old twins. Becoming trapped in the past is unproductive because it can only hold you back and negatively influence your choices, but becoming trapped in the future is pointless because you just never know where the road may lead you. My sense of self is wider than ever and I am content in not giving a damn for the sake of all of us.

Not giving a damn has also been vital to my career. As a young intern I used to fall back on my old habit of equating manic outpouring of energy with effectiveness. I became notorious in those early days of my medical career for working longer hours than anyone. I prided myself on it. Part of this was for financial reasons, but part was also for the impression of myself I wanted to convey. I could do more and work harder than anyone and I wanted the world to know it. If it also provided financial benefit, well so much the better. For much of my career I found this a hard habit to break. By the time I came to see reasonableness of not giving a damn I had become tangled up in schedules and obligations from which I found it very hard to escape. After nearly 20 years of both obstetrics and gynecology I realized that racing off in the middle of the night more often than not and surviving on caffeine during the day was not the right choice for me and my family. I didn't have enough time or energy for my children, and my health was beginning to suffer. I finally looked at my situation clearly and honestly and realized I had to stop obstetrics and curtail some of my surgical responsibilities. This would mean a significant reduction of income but I didn't give a damn. The right choice for me at the time was to connect more with my children and see to my own physical condition. It was the right choice for me at that moment and I still believe it is in this one.

I still perform surgery on a fairly regular basis, and it is in this context that I am most aware of the benefit to my work as a doctor that I not give a damn. It is not unusual that the several surgeons who needed to be hired to take up a fraction of the load I once carried consult me on an emergency basis when they find themselves in over their heads. I must admit that it feels somewhat satisfying to walk into the chaotic scene of a complicated surgical situation and calmly restore order. Most of the time the key to success is keeping your head when those about you are losing theirs. Panic, worry, regret, and self-image have no place in such a situation, as I have learned over the years. My experiences as a surgeon have played a large role in convincing me of the overall benefit of not giving a damn.

Running a private medical practice requires a physician to also be a small businessman. It is a well-known expression in the medical world that good physicians often make lousy business people. I believe this is true, and for good reason. A good physician will put his or her patients first and all business considerations second. This is, to a large extent, the way it should be. In my case, I never turn away a woman in need of gynecological care because her insurance isn't up to date and/or her financial situation makes it questionable if she will be able to pay. My responsibility is to serve the needs of my patients and I don't give a damn about anything else. There are always bills to pay and records to keep, but my best choice in any given moment will be to give my undivided attention and best treatment to the women who come to me for care. I can't imagine practicing medicine any other way. I can say from long experience that dealing with large hospitals, insurance companies, or medical organizations is another situation altogether. For them, giving a damn about things like profit seems to be the chief concern. But will tell you more about this another time.

Part of the reason that I made the decision to curtail my work hours was an awareness that my girth was expanding at an unhealthy rate. Lack of sleep means lack of exercise, and eating on the run means eating badly. Coupled with unhealthy amounts of caffeine, this is a recipe for physical disaster. I decided one day—really decided—that I needed to lose weight. Once I truly accepted my decision internally the rest was "easy." Sure, it's no fun feeling hungry, and making a habit of exercise is not easy at the beginning, but once the decision was well and truly made I had left myself no choice. The rest was a matter of details. I counted my calories and reduced from an alarming daily intake to something that would obviously result in loss of weight. Knowing that the body consumes muscle before fat, I started a regular exercise regimen to ensure my weight loss would be healthy and appropriate. Over the course of a year I lost over forty pounds and have kept it off for going on three years now. The hardest part was making that initial decision. I knew that simply wanting to be thinner was not the same as making a commitment to myself, so I didn't start until I was truly ready. Now I offer guidance and advice to my patients who want to lose weight themselves. I tell them that it all starts with them not giving a damn.

Many positive things start with not giving a damn. Through the many twists and turns and ups and downs of my life I have gradually come to realize that the most positive and successful things I have done—even the painful but necessary things—have come when I didn't give a damn. When I can avoid the traps of the past and future, when I disregard the irrelevant views of others, and when I clearly, honestly, and directly assess the choices in front of me at this very moment I tend to make the right ones more often than not. So can you.

CHAPTER 12

THE PRACTICAL GUIDE TO NOT GIVING A DAMN

Now that we've covered what it really means to not give a damn and how it applies to several areas of life, it is time to consider how you can stop giving a damn as a practical matter for yourself. Bear in mind that what follows is just my advice based on what we've discussed so far. At the end of the day, you need to make the best decisions for you in the current moment without giving a damn what I, or anyone else, says.

⁂

Avoid the traps

To avoid the traps of time, you need to come to terms with your past, present, and future and look at yourself clearly here and now. Regrets are not unusual; anyone who has seen something of life has probably experienced regret. However, it is not a useful feeling. Before you can make clear, honest decisions now you have to take a clear, honest look at what has come and who you have been in the past. Not every memory is a pleasant one, but dwelling on perceived failures in the past will only hold you back. Instead, look frankly at what has come before, and then relegate the past to the past where it belongs. No matter what may have happened in your past, by definition you cannot change it and if you allow it to control you present day decisions, you are trapped. Avoiding the pit of regret is difficult because it pulls on your sense of responsibility and accountability. In practical (and sometimes legal) terms you may have to pay in some way for what you have done in the past, but in emotional terms there is the danger that you will go on paying the same bill over and over forever. It's not easy to leave the past in the past, especially when there are weighty and significant events there, but failure to do so will only confound your present and restrict your future.

The past is not the only trap that needs to be avoided. There is also the trap of the present. What this amounts to is allowing non-essential influences to become a part of your decision making process. Do you really think your neighbors care what car you drive? Will your co-workers really care if you can or cannot discuss the popular TV show around the water cooler or regurgitate the latest box scores? Does anyone on earth care that you bought the latest electronic gadget, and if so will this benefit you in any way? Devoting one second of your life to the concerns of people who couldn't care less about you is supremely wasteful. Wear what you want to wear, eat what is good for you and also tasty, adjust your standard of living to fit your circumstances whatever they may be. Chances are, few outside your own family and friends give a damn about you anyway.

Focus on the here and now. Sit down and look at the choices in front of you this minute and make the best ones based on your own circumstances. This means opening those bills, choosing carefully what food you put in your body, being honest with your loved ones, and measuring the cost and benefit of your every decision. Make your choices and live your life as if this very moment will be your last. Doing your best as work and play, honoring your body, and loving your family as much as you possibly can are habits that can be adopted as easily as all the negative ones we know of. Live in and for this moment. Truly accepting the notion that this moment may be your last motivates more positive thought and behavior than you might believe.

Another dangerous trap is the future. The future is a slippery trap because it contains elements of the positive and the negative in equal measure. Fear of the future can immobilize you and prevent you from taking the reasonable chances necessary to achieve anything significant. Exaggerated optimism can lead you into to reckless behavior and unrealistic expectations. Either case interferes with clear and reasoned decision making. Only through clear, direct, honest decision-making can you come to the right choice, right here, right now.

⁂

Accept life for what it is

You are alive and you are going to die. In order to live your life to its fullest you have to appreciate it for what it is. Our corporeal existence in this world is necessarily of limited duration. No one escapes this reality no matter how many vitamins you take, dollars you donate, or if your head gets frozen in a jar next to Ted Williams. Take time to stop and consider who and what you are. Make the time—if even just a little—to reflect upon yourself or to just absorb the reality that you are in fact alive. Become aware of your breathing, feel your blood circulating, and allow your mind to just be at rest for a few moments. Most of us spend every minute of every day as if our brains were full of bees buzzing every which way, and at the end of the day we wonder why we need medications to get us to sleep. Give yourself a minute. Expand. Focus on nothing and everything for just a very short time. You will be amazed at how refreshing it is. When it comes to death, don't be afraid. Everyone dies, why pretend otherwise? Life is all about changes, and death is just the final one (as far as we can determine with cer-tainty). No one expresses terror at what came before they were born, but humanity has exerted an enormous amount of energy over the idea of what happens after we die. The price of admission to life is death. Don't fear it; allow the realization of it to make your life more meaningful.

⌘ ⌘ ⌘

Address financial issues

Don't hide from or deny issues pertaining to money. Avoiding financial issues will not make them go away, and under very few circumstances will they result in you going to jail if you are honest and direct about them. Open those bills. Pay the ones you can. Contact the ones you cannot pay and make arrangements. There are more options available than you might think when you are cringing from the accumulating pile of numbers flooding towards you. Make the choices and adjustments you must in order to deal with the reality that presents itself to you. Simplify, prioritize, and when you do get out from under the pile remember the lessons learned and avoid the lures of over-consumption and bad terms. Remember that the most foolish reason to wind up in a negative debt spiral is giving a damn what the neighbors think you should drive, wear, eat, or otherwise consume.

⁂

Manage your weight and your health

Lose the weight if you really want to. Obesity in the United States is a severe and "growing" problem. As a physician I am terribly concerned with what I see among my patients year to year. The ramifications of this rapidly expanding epidemic are many and significant. There are few medical conditions so severe that are so clearly and directly manageable by the behavior of patients. All it takes is a decision. Not wanting to make a decision, not feeling bad about not making a decision, not fantasizing about what a decision might mean, but actually making a decision. Once the decision is truly made and fully internalized the process of accomplishing the goal is relatively simple. Almost everyone knows how to do it, but a shockingly low number of people out of the total actually decide to do it. Read carefully: eat less and exercise more. Once you have truly, honestly, and completely made the decision it is all but done. It's not fun to be hungry, but it's a lot less fun to be sick.

⁂

Accept love

When you love, love completely and take it seriously. Love is not only a joy and the highest expression of the human condition, but it is also a great responsibility. When you love you actually take another into your own sense of self. You essentially abandon full autonomy of self in favor of an expanded notion of "me." This is something not to be entered into lightly. We have spent a lot of time talking about how you should not give a damn what others think about your decisions in the here and now. When you love someone they cease to be an "other" and become part of the "you" whose interests you are most concerned with at every moment. If you are not prepared to accept a person at that level then you don't really love them and it is much better to recognize that than to pretend otherwise.

Remember that love is a feeling and not a physical alteration and as such it is more subject to change. It can take a long time for a Redwood tree to die and fall down, but love can change remarkably quickly and with equal impact. If you don't keep your eyes open it's easy to get squashed.

⌘ ⌘ ⌘

Accept faith

Revel in your faith and all the comforts it provides you, but don't allow it to become a wedge between you and your fellow human beings. Faith is a building block of higher cognition and can challenge and inspire us in many ways. As long as we don't allow faith to become a weapon turned against us for division, manipulation, and exploitation then this powerful force can be used for the greater good. Regardless of the particular religious tradition, if any, into which your faith leads you, a clear and honest mind can derive great benefit from pondering the mysteries and reflecting on our place in the order of things. For people of science like myself, faith can be a tough pill to swallow but I know I don't have all the answers, and recognize the positive (and negative) effect faith has had on many of those around me.

See yourself in your loved ones

Cherish your family and recognize them for what they are. They are you. Family is an extension of yourself and as such becomes part of the "you" that is considered when you don't give a damn. Not every-one occupies the same place with -in your consciousness and not all family members are as integrally connected in your sense of self. Nonetheless, it is important to bear in mind the expanded responsibili-ties involved in not giving a damn when you are part of a family.

Above all, be aware of yourself and don't let negative, unproduc-tive, or unnecessary influences to affect your decision-making process. Keep outside influences where they belong, block out the noise, put your-self first, and make every decision for and of the here and now.

ACKNOWLEDGMENTS

This book would not have been possible without the aid, influence, and support of all the people in my life who have helped me reach the point where I felt I had something of value to offer to others. This includes a very long list of teachers, family, lovers, patients, mentors, friends, and enemies. All have contributed to making me who I am today. If anything I have written here is of value to anyone, all credit should go to them. My patients have not only formed the basis of my professional life, but have shaped my identity and taught me more than 100 years of medical school ever could. I would like to thank my mother, who has endured more and overcome greater obstacles than most people could believe. I am humbly aware of how much of what is good in my life I owe to her tireless sacrifice and support. I must thank my five children, who give my life meaning and purpose; for whom I live and would without hesitation die. Finally, I want to give all due recognition to my loving wife, who has blessed and saved my life in ways I could never do justice in words.

Made in the USA
Charleston, SC
15 February 2012